Applied Empathy

THE NEW LANGUAGE OF LEADERSHIP

MICHAEL VENTURA

TOUCHSTONE

New York   London   Toronto   Sydney   New Delhi

Touchstone
An Imprint of Simon & Schuster, Inc.
1230 Avenue of the Americas
New York, NY 10020

First Touchstone hardcover edition May 2018

TOUCHSTONE and colophon are registered trademarks of Simon & Schuster, Inc.

For information about special discounts for bulk purchases,
please contact Simon & Schuster Special Sales at 1-866-506-1949
or business@simonandschuster.com.

The Simon & Schuster Speakers Bureau can bring authors to your live event.
For more information or to book an event, contact the Simon & Schuster Speakers Bureau
at 866-248-3049 or visit our website at www.simonspeakers.com.

Manufactured in the United States of America

1 3 5 7 9 10 8 6 4 2

Library of Congress Cataloging-in-Publication Data has been applied for.

ISBN 978-1-5011-8285-3
ISBN 978-1-5011-8287-7 (ebook)

For Caroline and Darryl,
two of my greatest teachers

Contents

Introduction

Empathy is a squishy word. Sometimes it's confused with sympathy or misinterpreted as "being nice." That isn't empathy. Empathy is about understanding. Empathy lets us see the world from other points of view and helps us form insights that can lead us to new and better ways of thinking, being, and doing.

The words *business* and *empathy* are rarely used together—in fact, for some of us they might even sound oxymoronic, but there are incredible benefits to taking on others' perspectives in the context of our professional lives. That's what *Applied Empathy* is about. Empathy is not some out-of-reach mystical power. Instead it is a skill that each of us can make a part of our daily practice and ultimately bring into the organizations we serve.

This book presents a set of tools and ideas for applying empathy to:

- Understanding your customers' needs and improving your products and services by infusing them with rich, meaningful insights gleaned from a newfound perspective.
- Connecting and collaborating with your teams more effectively—understanding the skills and styles of each

1

person and how to get the most out of your interactions.

- Leading with a new awareness that will undoubtedly
aid you in not only understanding others better but,
perhaps more important, understanding the truest
aspects of your own self.

Applying empathy may seem obvious for one-to-one interactions, and it is a critical part of any good relationship, but it's
also a powerful advantage when applied at the business level to
gain perspective within your company's walls and in the world
within which the company operates.

There are countless instances in the business world where
companies have missed the opportunity to apply empathy, many
of them paying dearly for the oversight.

One of the most infamous was Xerox's fumbled opportunity to lead the personal computing industry. Back in the 1960s,
Xerox's 914 photocopier revolutionized the business world. At
the same time, the company's innovation facility, the Palo Alto
Research Center (PARC), was fast at work developing other new
and insightful products. One of those was the Xerox Alto, the
first fully functional personal computer. It had processing power,
a graphic interface, and even a mouse. So why isn't Xerox a computing juggernaut today?

In the 1970s, Xerox's leadership was largely focused on rak-
ing in the massive profits generated by the 914 photocopier—
which was not sold but leased to customers, who were charged per
page—instead of looking out into the world and using empathy
to sense the growing demand for personal computing. They didn't
do anything with the Alto or, frankly, with many of the other
great inventions that PARC was churning out. They were pre-

occupied with their current successes and uninterested in understanding the shifting consumer needs around them. As a result, they missed one of the greatest technology booms the business world has ever experienced.

Another more recent example of a lack of empathic leadership can be seen in the music industry's inglorious failure to participate in the digital music revolution. While executives stretched their travel and expense accounts to the max and obsessed over CD distribution deals with brick-and-mortar retailers, Napster and LimeWire were hard at work building a completely new, and more empathic, distribution system that aligned with consumers and their needs (though not empathic to the artists or the record industry they were disrupting). Missing that opportunity crushed the major music labels' business and gave rise to powerhouses such as Apple Music and Spotify.

Would empathy alone have saved those companies from disaster? It's hard to say. But had they applied empathy more meaningfully in their decision-making, they could have recognized new and innovative ways to lead their businesses into the next era.

Fortunately, plenty of companies *are* applying empathy to solve tough challenges and lead teams with new and powerful insight.

A darling of the start-up world, Warby Parker's meteoric growth can be closely mapped to its executives' clear understanding of the "grit" in the retail eyewear experience. Consumers weren't getting what they needed from any of the big players in the space, and Warby Parker's founders saw an opportunity to jump into the category offering a more human, service-oriented approach that has been voraciously embraced. (Full disclosure: we've worked with them and can attest to their empathic strengths firsthand.)

One of my favorite empathic thinkers is Elon Musk. He truly

understands the needs of the market and has proven to be a powerful innovator and entrepreneur who can apply his understanding to a variety of industries. Most recently, he's decided to take on the challenge of "soul-crushing traffic." His venture, The Boring Company, is solving this problem in an unexpected way. While everyone from Hollywood moviemakers to Ivy League–educated futurists has spent time imagining a world full of flying cars, Musk has taken his vision to a subterranean level, focusing instead on building a technologically advanced tunneling business designed to solve our increasingly gridlocked roadways by expanding them to the ground below us.

These companies and their leaders understand how to use empathy to look at problems differently and create solutions that not only disrupt conventions but use empathy as a powerful tool.

My own company, Sub Rosa, is a strategy and design studio that works with large, often complex corporations as well as progressive thinkers in government, entertainment, and the start-up world to help them evolve their businesses with empathy. We have worked with some of the world's most recognizable companies and leaders, and I'm proud that those clients have sought us out because we offer fresh solutions that support their need to explore, learn, and grow.

Our clients come to us because we can help them figure out who they truly are, what they are actually trying to accomplish, and, perhaps most important, show them how to take their goals or their businesses to a higher level.

- We've worked with countless CEOs and leadership teams to think differently about how empathy can ignite a spirit of creativity, innovation, and growth in the hearts and minds of their teams around the world.

- We've helped one of the world's most successful athletes understand himself and his brand with empathy—giving him a mission and vision that will take his career to new heights.
- We even brought empathy into the West Wing of the Obama White House, applying our thinking to a series of initiatives started by the first family to help bring a greater sense of understanding to our nation's indigenous people's rights and resources.

Empathy lets us better understand the people we are trying to serve and gives us perspective and insight that can drive greater, more effective actions. The seemingly magical quality of empathy is the connection it helps us form with other people. Some of us are born with an overwhelming degree of empathy, while others are callous or even blind to the perspectives of others. The rest of us fall somewhere in between. But empathy is more than just a natural talent; it can also be a process, a learned skill, developed and applied when and where needed.

Applied Empathy begins with my journey of discovery, one that led to an early client assignment that helped those of us at Sub Rosa define who we are and how we approach our work. Through that project and others like it, we developed what we call *Empathic Archetypes* along with an understanding of the complex world within ourselves that we term the *Whole Self*. After establishing this baseline of empathic thinking, I will show you how leaders manifest empathy and how they encourage it in others. From there, we'll continue to dive deeper into empathy, looking at its role in the world around us. We'll look at its timeless nature, drawing from lessons of the past, present, and future; its application in the context of some of today's tough business challenges; how it can play a role in evolving our own realities; and why now, more than perhaps at any other time in human history, we need it to solve the challenges lying before us.

Our best work demands empathy, and that means each of us must be able to call on it when needed, regardless of mood or circumstances. To help elevate empathy from a buzzword to a reliable, repeatable, and responsive tool, I've taken all the lessons and thinking we've amassed on this topic and poured them into this book. May it bring to you the same appreciation for understanding it has brought to me.

CHAPTER ONE

The Way In

"If you don't get into trouble, you'll never learn how to get out of it." That was the advice a friend's dad gave me back in 2003. I was twenty-three years old, had a little less than two years of advertising experience, and had just lost my job. I wasn't sure about the risk I was about to take, but I was ready to meet whatever challenges I was about to face head-on.

With faith in myself and the people around me, I decided to found my own company, a design agency in New York City that would grow into the business I run today. The risk of starting my own business would be the first of many challenges I'd encounter as an entrepreneur. More than a decade later, my company, Sub Rosa, has worked with some of the world's largest and most important brands and organizations, from Google, Johnson & Johnson, and Nike to TED, the United Nations, and even the Obama White House.

I often say we work as translators. Companies and organizations bring us in to help them establish their vision, share their message, or bring something new to the world. We work with them to create a plan, to see a path toward what they want to become, and then we help enact it. Sub Rosa is full of talented people—designers, strategists, technologists, producers, and researchers, to name a few.

We are the "land of misfit toys," mixed with a drawer full of Swiss Army knives. Perhaps paradoxical for some, most of the time our best work leads to our own obsolescence. But we see that as a good thing. In essence, we solve problems using an approach we call Applied Empathy, and through this process we empower companies to explore, learn, and grow along with us. It's work I'm insanely proud to spend my days doing.

So how did we get here? I had the dubious fortune of graduating from college in 2002, just when the dot-com bubble burst. It was not an easy time to get a job, and there were very few entry-level positions to be found. Whenever I did find an opening and applied, I invariably lost it to people who already had a few years of experience. It was disheartening for a wide-eyed twenty-one year old who was ready to take on the world if only someone would give him a chance.

Eventually I landed a job at a boutique advertising agency as a sort of utility player, shifting among office administrator, project manager, art department intern, and executive assistant for some of the leadership team. The job quickly exposed me to many facets of the industry, and I was able to see the ins and outs of running a company. I sponged up everything I could. In this role, I saw how important it was to understand the people around me—my bosses, colleagues, vendors, and clients—if I wanted to serve them better and get my work done effectively.

Luckily, I've always felt I had a knack for understanding people and situations. When I was a kid, I didn't have a word for it, but we're talking about empathy. No one gave me a lesson in it as I was headed out to the playground, and no one said it was something I needed to learn. But looking back at my childhood and my teenage years that followed, I recall an ability to innately sense when others were having a hard time or wrestling with a problem.

My parents tell me that when I was around ten years old, they asked what I wanted to be when I grew up, and I told them an "idea man." They had no clue where I came up with this. "Idea man" wasn't a career most ten-year-olds were thinking about. But something inside me knew I loved solving problems and using my mind to come up with ways of moving things in a better direction.

I know this makes me sound like a dork, but I was the guy who tried to help the overwhelmed substitute teacher calm down the class. It wasn't that I had sympathy for her, but I did understand what she was going through, and I wanted to help. After school I could tell when my friends were struggling with a crisis of confidence at the free-throw line or in a relationship with someone, and I always wanted to lend a hand and tried to help them see the problem from a different perspective. In the high school lunchroom, I bounced from table to table, hanging with jocks, goths, musicians, stoners, AP students, and everyone in between. I always found ways of connecting with virtually everyone, sometimes even bringing groups together.

Don't get the idea that I was the Dalai Lama or something. I wasn't brokering peace deals during recess or volunteering my time in the local orphanage. I was a fairly typical middle-class kid growing up in suburban New Jersey. But I knew I was good at understanding people and seeing things from their point of view, and that was something I loved to share. It made others feel comfortable. And it was something I would always honor as an integral part of me.

During my short-lived stint at the ad agency, I relied on that skill a lot. Understanding other people's jobs, their motivations and goals, was critical to doing my job well. I learned a lot of practical skills in those eighteen months, but I was also discovering a lot of what I didn't want for my future. Too many people in the working world seemed to be going through the motions. I saw emotional blindness everywhere. I saw people do their jobs, punching in at 9:00 a.m. and out at 6:00 p.m. most days.

Of course, in the ad business there were plenty of late nights and deadlines and hemming and hawing at the bar after work. But generally speaking, I felt a lack of purpose. It was a job, and that's fine—not everyone needs to derive their life's satisfaction from their job. Some people work to earn a living so they can pursue their passions elsewhere. But that wasn't for me. I wanted a job that *was* an expression of my passion. I wanted to fix problems. I wanted to help people better understand themselves and those around them. As my ten-year-old self had said, I wanted to be an idea man.

After I had worked at the advertising firm for eighteen months, the universe stepped in and gave me a nudge. The company didn't wait for me to decide if I should leave; it decided for me. I was fired without warning. The CEO thought I wasn't spending enough time on the executive assistant part of the job, and I was out. No formal review, no negative feedback for me to try to correct. Just "This isn't working" and "Good-bye." In retrospect, it was the gift of a lifetime, though I definitely didn't feel that way when it happened.

There I was, unemployed in New York City, helplessly watching my meager savings evaporate. The job market was still down, and I was having trouble finding another job fast enough. At the same time, my college girlfriend and I broke up, and the rent-controlled apartment we shared was going condo. I couldn't live there much longer, and before I knew it, I was doing the thing that pretty much every twenty-three-year-old dreads: I moved home with my parents.

Meanwhile, my friend Albert was withering away as a software engineer at Lehman Brothers. We were both stuck and needed to figure out how to change our lives. One night over a beer, I told Albert I had a plan. Remember, this was the early 2000s, a time when every company was looking to build a website, and I looked around and decided I'd learned just enough to be a little dangerous. I told Albert I was going to start a design firm. And I wanted him to join me.

Our resources were incredibly limited. We each had a laptop and some cheap business cards we printed ourselves. I borrowed my mom's car and drove into the city, where Albert and I networked with potential clients. Even though those were the earliest days of our business, we knew we had something many other firms didn't have. We had an innate knowledge of the Web because we'd grown up using it. On the surface, we looked like a Web design shop. But we were actually much more, an empathy-wielding problem-solving studio, even if we hadn't realized it yet.

Of course, we probably looked like a couple of kids playing grown-up, wearing suits to meetings and talking like we had heard other execs talk: "omnichannel strategies," "digital ecosystems," and whatever other catchphrase *du jour* was being bandied about in the trades that week. But underneath that schmoozy business veneer, I like to think we stood out because of our honest desire to connect with people and help them solve the problems they were facing.

We drummed up a few clients before I even told my parents what I was doing. When I sheepishly came clean to them one night, worried that they'd tell me I needed to get a "real job" or something, they surprised me.

They told me, "You don't have your own family to provide for. Or a mortgage. You can live cheap. Now's the time to give this a shot!"

That shouldn't have surprised me, because my mom and dad

had always been my biggest supporters in whatever I was doing, but I was nervous about the risk and was subconsciously looking for someone to tell me I was crazy. They did the exact opposite, and that encouragement played a pivotal role in nudging my dream into reality.

Soon enough we were making a name for ourselves, and the studio grew. We took on partners and landed some bigger clients, and I began to realize that if we wanted to differentiate ourselves as an agency, we couldn't just tell people what they wanted to hear. We would listen, we would connect, and we would always try to see the work through the perspective of the client and the audience it was trying to reach and not just offer one-sided solutions. It didn't take long before we had built a reputation as a place companies came to when they wanted to learn how to create real engagement with their customers. We were becoming known as a company that could understand audiences authentically.

The agency was getting bigger than any of us was ready to handle. We were up to around forty people, and we'd added new services such as experiential marketing (back then it was called guerrilla marketing), as well as content creation. I was exhausted, and my body was literally breaking down under the pressure. I started doing whatever I could to cope: drinking, smoking, staying out till all hours, taking whatever upper or downer I needed to avoid thinking about the next day's mess.

By 2008, the financial crisis was looming, clients' purse strings were tightening, and the company was on shaky ground. My partners wanted to go elsewhere, but I still saw potential in what we'd started. But I couldn't keep up at that pace. Something had to give.

That's when I threw out my back. I was changing the water cooler in the studio, and the next thing I knew I was lying on the floor, the water jug glugging its contents all over me. I had herniated three discs in my lumbar spine. I ended up in the hospital, and the doctors said I needed surgery. The surgery wouldn't fix everything, but it would help the pain. I couldn't accept that diagnosis. I ambled out and went to an acupuncturist. It was my first visit to an Eastern medicine doctor. One session certainly didn't cure me, but I felt a little better. I continued seeing the acupuncturist and combined that with other forms of Eastern medicine as a way of repairing my battered body. That introduced me to an entirely new way of understanding and caring for myself. My body, mind, and spirit all needed healing, and I knew this was the start of a long journey.

I began to delve deeply into the sacred wisdom of indigenous cultures. Mesoamerican shamans, Chinese traditional medicine practitioners, Native American tribal elders, Indian yogis—all of those and more opened their world to me and helped me better connect with myself. My back was soon mended, and my spirit had stumbled onto a new path.

A NEW PATH

In 2009, inspired by the ancient wisdom I was learning and a desire to integrate it into my work, I restructured our company, downsizing to a small core team and parting ways with my partners, who were ready to move on. I rebranded the company Sub Rosa. The term is Latin, literally "under the rose"; its colloquial meaning was that of conversations had in confidence.

The work we do for clients is modern and state of the art, but indigenous wisdom is fundamental to our practice. We don't incorporate it overtly because we know some folks aren't going to jibe with what might seem like abstract philosophy—at least at first—but it inspires our thinking and drives the way we approach problems and reach solutions.

But before we could get to where we are today, we had to discover who we were and what kind of organization we wanted to be. We'd built a good foundation doing work for clients like Kiehl's and Absolut Vodka, helping them build programs that connected with influential consumers and thought leaders. We'd worked hand in hand with Levi's to create a campaign that established the brand's vision for its next chapter and helped it contribute in a meaningful way to local communities it cared for deeply. That was the kind of stuff we loved doing, and our successes helped establish our competency as equal parts strategic thinkers and creative doers.

We had worked with General Electric on a number of projects, ranging from its Ecomagination program to helping evolve the way the brand participates with influential thought leaders. Our partnership had developed into one of deep mutual respect based on the work we had done together. For that reason, the company came to us when it needed help with a new and complex challenge involving its medical imaging business. We were excited to continue working with the company; what we didn't know was that the assignment would provide us with an opportunity to define who we are and what we do. Looking back, it was a critical turning point for us.

It began when General Electric's chief marketing officer, Beth Comstock, presented us with an extraordinary challenge. "Today," she said, "GE is lagging in the medical imaging business. We want to be the best."

Of course they did. They're GE. You don't last long at General Electric if you're comfortable anywhere but in first place.

The company wanted someone to help it spur rapid change and innovation throughout its massive medical imaging business, which included CAT and PET scanners, MRIs, ultrasound scanners, and mammography systems. These medical investigative tools provide physicians with vital information about what's going on inside their patients' bodies, and they had become an important part of GE's health care revenue. The company could not afford to slip behind in this area, and their leadership believed we were the right partner to help reinvigorate the business.

I was proud that our studio of less than twenty people was being tapped for an assignment like this, but before I could even start beaming, Beth threw two conditions at us. "We can give you only five months," she said, "and you can't propose any direct product changes because that won't move our business in the right direction quickly enough." GE had already been working to develop new imaging technology and improved form factors for its machines, but those changes wouldn't be implemented for several years. They wanted to spur growth faster than that, and we were the team charged with finding a way to do so.

She also told us the company wanted to keep our scope narrow enough to be successful, so it wanted us to focus specifically on its mammography business and to use what we learned there for the other imaging tools.

"Okay," I said to myself. "All we have to do is completely reinvent the mammography experience in the next five months and help drive growth throughout the whole business."

It's a good thing I wasn't in an MRI machine at that moment, because my brain probably looked as though it were having a ministroke. My palms had started sweating, and a pasty dryness had formed in my mouth. I swallowed hard and said we were ready to take on the job.

We got back to the studio, and all of us took a moment to catch our breath. I gathered the team to begin figuring out what to do first. It turned out that none of the women on our team had ever had a mammography, meaning that we lacked any firsthand knowledge. In essence, we were being charged with improving something none of us had ever experienced—and for that matter couldn't actually change (though some of our team members did go for a mammography to understand the experience better). What's more, even though theoretically all of us could sit in a chair and go through a simulated scan, that wouldn't help us truly understand what a woman was going through when she was being tested for something as frightening as breast cancer.

GE's confidence in us and its belief that we were capable of handling a challenge like this spoke volumes to me. I had no intention of letting the company down. But to do the job right, we would have to refine our process, and that was where our empathic methodology was truly born.

PUTTING EMPATHY INTO PRACTICE

We had already been using empathy in our work with clients, but we hadn't started using the word *empathy* to describe our methods. You could say we'd been practicing empathy, even if we hadn't been calling it that. In the end, it became clear to all of us how much empathy played a role in our work improving GE's mammography business.

To deliver for our client, we needed to immerse ourselves immediately. We knew right from the get-go that we needed to meet patients directly and connect with their stories. We needed to understand what goes on when you get a mammogram—not just technically but emotionally. And we needed to define what success for GE would look like.

We started by mapping out the entire process. The first thing we discovered was that GE's business was focused on selling its machines to hospitals, not interacting with patients. That seemed like a rich opportunity. How could we incorporate what we learned about patients into the way GE managed its relationships with hospitals? We started to realize that if GE provided superior patient experiences through its involvement with hospitals, hospitals would have better patient feedback. Better patient feedback means higher-ranked hospitals. And in the end, if patients and hospitals are happy with the experience of a GE product, they are more inclined to grow their relationship.

That was a path we wanted to explore. We began to meet with patients, doctors, technicians, and others in the mammography screening process. Listening carefully, it became clear that the only way to get the women to open up and talk about their personal, intimate experiences was to create a warm, safe space for them.

We saw that a phone call, even an interview in an office setting, wouldn't provide the necessary level of comfort and safety. That led us to realize how important the setting for our work would be. It wasn't just about the place where we did our interviewing but also the actual rooms in which mammographies were performed. We realized we needed to create that sort of space—a safe space in which to share conversation and learn firsthand from the people we were engaging in the work. That was when things started to get interesting.

We went looking for a space that would promote natural, authentic conversation about a sometimes scary, sometimes uncomfortable, always personal subject. Eventually we took over a vacant retail storefront in New York's SoHo neighborhood, a trendy shopping district that's also fairly residential. To some, the "obvious" home for the space might have been near a major hospital or in an office building a few floors up from the bustling city streets, but we wanted to be right in the middle of where patients lived and worked. We wanted to be something they could "happen upon" and where they could have a conversation. We wanted to be in their comfort zone and meet the participants in the research halfway.

Over a few short weeks, we outfitted the space with comfortable seating, a hospitality area where we could host larger groups, and a research library stocked with books and information about mammography and cancer treatments. We built demo waiting and exam rooms to prototype and test new ideas. We now had a living laboratory, where we discovered the value of live experimentation and testing.

It wasn't a real, functioning mammography clinic, and the women knew that. That probably wouldn't have been possible, considering the time we had for the project, nor would it have been practical. Still, portions of the space were designed to evoke the *experience* of getting an exam, to help participants feel the emotions they might feel when getting an actual mammography. We did that so we could get participants into the right headspace and so we could have meaningful conversations with them.

At the same time, we struck up a conversation with our friends at the design consultancy IDEO. We knew the team there had also done work in this space and that with a challenge this big and broad, having their medical research background would help us move more efficiently through our research.

With the space finished, and our partners and schedule all

aligned, we opened the doors and began inviting in our first round of visitors: women who regularly had mammograms, breast cancer survivors, doctors, nurses, and product engineers.

We'd trained the team to be present and to inhabit that space fully, fostering a safe environment for difficult conversations. We had to be sure that anyone we wanted to interview encountered people who were fully engaged and supportive. We knew how important it was to focus on understanding how a woman experiences a mammogram, from the moment she schedules her appointment until she leaves the facility after it's performed. We invited all types of women into the space. We had women from different socioeconomic groups. We had devoutly religious women sitting alongside atheists. We had senior citizens who had had mammograms before, chatting with women who were about to have their first screening. We did everything we could to open up the conversation and learn as much as the participants would share.

Over the first few weeks, we started to feel genuinely connected to our guests. They were coming back day after day, and they chatted with us and opened up about some of the most challenging aspects of their lives. As trust grew among all of us, we saw opportunities to push further, letting go of assumptions and asking probing, often more ambitious and deeper questions.

We wanted to know what it was like for patients in the days leading up to their screening. What were they thinking about when they went to bed at night? What were they concerned about? A group of women agreed to video journal their experiences in the days leading up to their mammography. They spoke to the camera in a way they couldn't speak to anyone else. They were raw and honest and open about their fears. Some had family histories of breast cancer and were worried about what they might find. A few had already found lumps in their breasts and were concerned that these could be cancerous.

We quickly learned how little attention had been paid to patients' experiences. And the more we connected empathically with the women's stories, the more we began to see the challenges they faced on their journey.

A mammogram is a commonly used method of detecting a cancerous growth in a woman's breast. Generally speaking, doctors recommend that most women over the age of forty get screened every twelve months. Breast cancer moves quickly, and early detection matters greatly for a woman's chance of survival. But statistics told us that not all women have a mammogram as regularly as they should, and it was important for us to discover why.

Early on, we found out that the number one thing women hate about a mammogram is the pain of the procedure. This wasn't terribly surprising, since during a conventional mammogram, two flat panels compress the breast tissue as flat as possible so that the machine can perform with the highest level of effectiveness. It's only for a few moments, but it's not fun. As a result, nine months later, when it's time to reschedule, some women delay. Nine months slip to twelve, twelve become fifteen . . . and fifteen might be too long. That pattern, we came to find, was all too common.

The pain was a direct result of the form and function of the machine itself—and we had already been told that we couldn't change the machine. But the pain of the procedure was a big problem and one that needed our attention. Our only recourse was to discover what other parts of the experience we could fix as a way of addressing the issue of pain from a new angle.

At the same time, we were having conversations about the other elements of the exam experience. One thing we heard frequently was that women hated the hospital gowns: the cheap material, the opening in the back. They were immodest. They didn't feel nice. The list went on and on. Tellingly, one woman referred to them as "the ones they give sick people." Those conversations revealed that there were plenty of opportunities to improve the overall experience—not only the gowns but also the language that caused patients to see a mammogram as a "dreadful" experience, rather than a helpful "health maintenance" procedure akin to an annual physical. That informed recommendations we would ultimately make regarding the literature given to patients in advance of the screening, as well as training for hospital staff in order to speak differently about the procedure.

At that point, we realized that many of the elements we were discussing didn't stem from GE and its business directly, but in order to solve this problem, we needed to look at those elements and see how they *could* become part of GE's business.

We continued our research into the environmental and service design elements of the patient experience, and we soon discovered that the patients hated the waiting rooms. Out-of-date magazines, ugly art, receptionists who treated patients like cattle instead of active participants in their own health. To say the rooms had been designed without any consideration of how patients would react to them would imply that they had been designed at all. The rooms we saw in our field research felt more like left-over spaces into which someone had put some badly upholstered chairs and a pump bottle of Purell. We could easily make changes there.

Keeping the importance of early detection in our minds, we knew we couldn't let minor things such as ugly gowns and crappy reading material continue to influence the overall experience and perhaps keep women from getting screened regularly. We also found that women avoid getting screened for reasons that are more serious than the gowns and waiting rooms. We heard things such as "My insurance doesn't cover it" or "I can't find time in my day." But some responses were emotionally deeper than others—statements such as "I have three family members who died of breast cancer. I hate seeing that exam on my calendar. It feels like an appointment with death." It became increasingly clear that many women were traumatized well before the exam even started.

If we were going to recommend changes to the gowns, improvements to the waiting areas or the scheduling process, and refinements to the language used by technicians, nurses, and doctors, it would require commitment, not just from GE but from hospitals and their staffs. To create that commitment, we would need to prove that making changes to those things could affect the overall experience. Even after all we had learned, we decided we were still too narrowly focused. Talking to doctors, patients, engineers, and caregivers was a start, but we needed to seek broader insights and find ways of improving the other parts of a mammography experience. We'd spoken to the usual suspects. It was time to bring in some unusual ones.

We invited in two brands that were already expert at creating warm environments and inviting products for women: Victoria's Secret and Kiehl's. We asked them to help us think through the reimagining of the waiting rooms, changing rooms, and mammography gowns. As we designed new and improved prototypes and made other changes to the nonclinical aspects of the mammography experience, we tested them in our space, asking visitors to go through mock exams and tell us how the changes affected their experience.

Pushing that sort of thinking further, we started talking with a whole host of other groups willing to lend their perspectives to our work. We brought in religious leaders, female designers and technologists, and documentarians expert at drawing out personal stories from their subjects. Our interaction with them was exceedingly valuable, highlighting insights derived from each of their unique perspectives and helping us think differently about ways we might reengineer the experience for the patients and, ultimately, help GE to think differently about its business as a whole.

OUR PROCESS TURNS UP THE HEAT

Perhaps the most astounding of our solutions came from a simple but constant complaint from many patients. The second biggest factor patients negatively cited about the procedure, after the memory of pain, was the room temperature. More than three-quarters of the women we spoke to told us that the exam rooms were uncomfortably cold. Now, was that alone driving their decision on whether to schedule a screening? Probably not. But it was coming up too often for us to ignore. We had to consider it from an empathic perspective. If more than three-quarters of the people we spoke to cited discomfort with the room's temperature, we needed to understand that problem further. So we decided to ask the technicians who actually conducted the test: Why was it always so cold in the exam room?

We learned that the exam room temperatures are set in accordance with the machinery guidelines. We spoke to the engineers who'd actually designed the machines and they told us that the optimal temperature for the life span of the machines is around 65° Fahrenheit.

That's cold—especially when you're wearing a flimsy gown and a stranger is squeezing your breast between two cold metal panels. We asked more questions and weren't surprised to learn that none of the people we interviewed had given much thought to the patient's comfort. It wasn't that they didn't care about the patient, but it wasn't their job to consider the patient. Their primary concerns were the machinery, the procedure, and the test results. But if women hate the test so much that they don't get it done regularly, what good is it?

We asked the (seemingly) obvious question: What if the room were slightly warmer? Would that adversely impact the machine or the exam?

It turns out, not so much. We ran a test with Memorial Sloan Kettering Cancer Center and our partners at IDEO. We brought in volunteers who had received a mammogram recently and asked the technicians to screen them again at a warmer temperature. We hypothesized that many of the women who had found the procedure painful would complain less when it was performed at a more comfortable temperature. We were thrilled to be right. We saw a double-digit decrease in the complaints of pain! That was just one small change, and it had already made patients substantially more comfortable during exams.

But that wasn't even the most significant finding. By increasing the temperature of the room by only 10 degrees, our test showed that the efficacy of the exam *increased* significantly.

That's right, a warmer room not only produced fewer complaints of pain, it also helped technicians and doctors detect more cancer cells in the breast tissue. When the room is warmer, the patient is more relaxed, which in turn keeps muscle tissue from tensing up, thereby allowing more rays to travel through the breast tissue and the test to be performed with greater clarity.

How had that simple change been overlooked for so long? It was no one's fault, really. No one had ever taken a holistic look at the experience and poked and prodded at the findings the way we did. We were being curious. We were trying to understand. And in that pursuit of understanding each element in the process, we found an opening. We found something so minor yet at the same time so major it might actually save lives.

We were elated and began to develop a whole new approach to the business, which we would share with our clients at GE. We took our findings to them and proposed that they grow their business by doing more than simply selling their product to hospitals and leaving it at that. They needed to take into consideration every aspect of the exam outside the exam equipment itself—from the terminology used by the staff to the gowns, the temperature, the lighting, and perhaps even the scent of the room. For GE, that meant a combined product/service offering, which ultimately became known as GE Imaging Centers—physical environments tailored to improving the comfort and well-being of patients.

That was something they had never considered. In essence, we were telling them that the way to improve their imaging business was not just by selling machines but by providing services that put their machines into the best, most empathically designed environments possible.

After our full presentation to the people at GE, we held our breath—waiting for their reaction. They smiled and said that our work was exactly the sort of thing they had been hoping we'd uncover, and all of us shared a moment of relief and pride. As a next step, they asked us to attend the annual meeting of the Radiological Society of North America, a trade convention being held on a subzero Thanksgiving weekend in Chicago. (An unempathic time and place for many conference attendees, but so be it.) Despite having to cut our holiday weekend short, we were pretty stoked because we were going there with some big news, and to make it even more exciting, it was being presented by a pretty powerful spokesman for our work, GE's chairman, Jeff Immelt.

Mr. Immelt was scheduled to give the keynote address, and during one part of his talk, he would tell the story of our experiment and announce the new offering to the room full of hospital and clinic managers. As soon as his speech was finished, GE's people started receiving inquiries, and before they knew it, they were signing up customers for the new service on the spot. That was completely unexpected. They'd assumed they'd get some inquiries, perhaps a hit or two in the trade media, but orders right there in the room? It was amazing to see it happen. Over the next few years, the business continued to grow and evolve as GE became more invested in the category and its emphasis on the power of empathy to solve problems for their customers.

In a larger sense, I believe that our work with GE helped change the way the organization thinks about its customers in all categories of its business. It was enormously gratifying to realize that we helped our client solve a complex challenge and expand its reach, but just as significantly, we helped to improve the mammography experience—which we hope has led to an improvement in the well-being of many people.

GOING WHERE EMPATHY TAKES YOU

That's the thing about this sort of work. You never really know what's going to happen when you start, but as you dive in and trust your empathic instincts and intuition, you are led into exciting new territories. For us, the work gave us a powerful foundation in our Applied Empathy approach. We didn't know it at the time, but while we were testing our thinking and prototyping our work, we were also discovering our true north.

Years later, I would look back at that assignment and see it as our origin story. At the time we were just doing what we innately knew best. But somewhere further down the road, we'd proudly see that important work as the start of everything that was to come.

CHAPTER 1 EXERCISES

Establishing Perspective

Honing your ability to view a situation from a perspective other than your own is one of the first things you must do to gain a stronger sense of empathy. The challenge comes in dropping your biases and points of view, which will free you to truly "see" from someone else's vantage.

To begin, take a moment to identify an issue you are trying to solve. It can be a personal or a professional challenge.

Some workplace examples might include:
- How can I build a better product for our customers?
- What is the smartest way to grow my organization?
- Who are the people I need on my team in order to be successful?

Or personal questions such as:
- Why do I have a hard time communicating my emotions to my partner?
- How can my family connect to each other on a deeper level?
- What do my friends rely on me for the most?

Once you've identified the right question, you'll want to establish three (or more) different perspectives you can use to evaluate it from new angles.

For example, if I were to take "How can I build a better product for our customers?" I might consider:

- My own perspective
- My customers' perspective
- My competitors' perspective

You will discover distinct insights as you consider the question from different perspectives. Let's say I'm a smartphone manufacturer and I want to improve my product. I might think I should increase its functionality, but it turns out that my customers care more about paying a lower price than having more features. Or perhaps I think the phone would be improved by faster speed, but then I discover that my competitors' greatest concern is that we have a more powerful design capability.

If I were to pursue this from only my perspective, I would focus on increasing the smartphone's functionality and speed. But taking into account the perspectives of my customers and my competitors, I realize that I need to deliver a more affordable product that continues to push the limits of good design while also fulfilling the function that I believe is right for the product.

Considering a question from multiple perspectives will help you make more well-rounded and better decisions.

Play around with the idea of perspectives. The "personal/ customer/competitor" configuration is just one of many you can devise. You might find that some problems benefit from being viewed through another set of points of view, such as "colleague/ elder/child."

You may find you need to do some research to understand the different perspectives. Talk to your customers or your competitors. Read articles or watch content that you think different audiences might consume. Play the part. Embody their point of view. Think of it as part ethnography and part method acting.

There's no wrong way to do this. Experiment with a variety of perspectives; just be sure they are varied enough that they cause you to step outside of your own point of view.

CHAPTER TWO

The Seven Faces of Empathy

"I suppose it is tempting," the renowned psychologist Abraham Maslow said, "if the only tool you have is a hammer, to treat everything as if it were a nail." We all have cognitive biases—pesky predilections that keep us from acting rationally and get in the way of our growth.

Think about it: when you're tackling a problem that's in your sweet spot, something you know how to do and have been doing for years, you can pretty easily find your way toward a viable solution, even if there are times when you risk the folly Maslow warns us about. But what happens when the problem is outside of your perspective or skill set? Typically we reach for our quickest, most facile tools—observation, deduction, cleverness—things that have helped us get by in the past. But often, big problems require greater perspective and deeper understanding to solve them, and this is where Applied Empathy comes in.

Unfortunately, few of us have received a formal education in empathy, and as adults, we end up intuitively feeling our way through to solutions based on our prior experiences and skills. That's not necessarily wrong, and many of us get by that way, but when empathy is overlooked, we are missing a key ingredient that can prove enormously helpful as we build our careers. Things get hairy when we face a challenge that requires us to get outside of ourselves and see the world from a different perspective. We feel uncomfortable, and as humans, we generally avoid the problems we don't understand. That often leaves us at a professional (and sometimes existential) standstill.

Early on in the development of our Applied Empathy philosophy, I started noticing where empathy was missing. You can fault the easy ones like the DMV or the local post office, but I also saw a lack of empathy in retail stores that treat customers dismissively—as an inconvenience to a sales associate busily engaged in an Instagram bender. I also saw it in the way some airlines and doctors' offices interact with their clientele—absent any sense of human connection or empathy for what an individual might be going through.

A few professions—social work, counseling, caregiving— already lean quite heavily on empathy as a job requirement, but for most career paths, empathy isn't mandatory; it's not sought out by human resource teams in the recruitment process, and hiring managers don't make it a priority. As my team and I started to see empathy become a foundational part of our work, we began to wonder if that "muscle" could be trained—if we could intentionally improve our empathy and refine its capacity to play a role in everything we do. We even asked if the ability to be empathic could be (re)awakened, even if it has atrophied.

I've come to wholeheartedly believe that everyone has the ability to do this, but I've learned that making this happen requires us to get back in touch with different parts of ourselves, different ways of being and showing up in the world.

I recognize that empathy sounds great, and of course everyone wants to be perceived as an empathic person. However, what we've discovered is that using empathy in your work often makes it harder, not easier. You have to listen, and you might not like what you hear. Real empathy, deep understanding and connection, is tough to create and even tougher to maintain day after day.

That was not an easy realization for me to come to, and it doesn't make empathy an easy thing to pitch. But it is worth the effort. I wish I could say I woke up one morning during our GE assignment and exclaimed, "The reason this is working is that we are using empathy to drive our problem-solving!" But it didn't happen like that.

EMPATHY IN APPLICATION

When we took on the GE mammography project, Sub Rosa was growing quickly. We were midstride on our path to fifty people. We were moving so fast that we didn't have a chance to hit "pause" and closely analyze what we were doing. We didn't have a deep understanding of all the elements at play in our work, and admittedly, we hadn't had a chance to crystallize a sense of our methodology. We were simply living it.

As we were finishing the mammography assignment, we continued to take on new projects from companies that were looking to tackle all sorts of challenges. Sometimes they were focused on corporate culture and change management. Other times, they were asking us to establish or reorient their brand in order to connect with their audiences more readily. We were "building the plane while we flew it," as the expression goes. But throughout that time, we were honing our practice of empathy and refining our thinking and problem-solving skills.

About a year later, the other leaders in the company and I realized we needed to have a better understanding of our underlying philosophy—essentially, how we do what we do. Having worked with so many clients going through their own growth spurts, we knew how valuable it would be to take the time to do a proper assessment of our company, its culture, and its processes in order to establish a clear point of view. After all, we were the company our clients had partnered with to do that kind of work. We decided to make ourselves our own best client. We pulled together a team of some of our best and brightest people. We drew up a scope, one that was similar to the type of assignment we used with our own clients, and we got to work.

Our first step was to examine our best client case studies and ask what we'd done well and why it was so effective. The GE mammography assignment was one my colleagues and I dug into intensely. We knew it shone a light on our ability to delve deeply into a situation, to understand it from all sides, and to use that insight—that empathic understanding—as a way of pushing through a problem and into a solution. We believed that if we studied that case and others like it, we would unearth something powerful—our own empathy origin story.

IT'S ABOUT TO GET PERSONAL

During that time, my own personal reflections on empathy became more and more apparent. I am a person who's pretty open and unafraid of self-work. I've studied with all sorts of gurus and masters, though many wouldn't refer to themselves by such haughty titles. I've also gained a greater understanding of my inner self through analysis and therapy, as well as a host of spiritual and alternative medicine practices. All of those efforts have helped me get closer to my inner self. And all of those things, every last one of them, were helpful in preparing me to better understand my own relationship to empathy because they had given me a more diverse perspective and capacity to understand myself and others from many sides.

I began looking for moments when my thoughts and actions were coming from an empathic place and realizing how often, to my disappointment, they were not. For instance, you may be surprised to hear that I am a linear, methodical thinker. Yes, I'm a creative at heart, and I spend a lot of my day cooking up ideas for clients that help solve their problems. But I have a process that isn't conducive to working off the cuff. If you throw me into a room with zero preparation and give me some markers and a whiteboard, I'm probably going to sit there staring at it for an hour or two before anything happens.

That's not so for a lot of the creatives I know. They can dive straight in and spitball ideas endlessly. I need to more fully understand a situation before I can do that. I need to see the bigger picture. I need to do some research. I need to talk with a few people and hear their perspectives. Otherwise I feel as though the ideas I generate are just built on "Wouldn't it be cool if . . ." propositions with little meaning. I want, and expect, more than that from myself and from the work my team produces.

One day my colleagues asked me to join an impromptu brainstorm. I was paired with a few other collaborators to quickly ideate a solution for a new client we were courting. They started firing out ideas and landing thoughts on the board, and I noticed my discomfort level start to rise. I was feeling adrift. I was aware of how little I understood the problem, the client's needs, and the audience it wanted to reach. That greatly hampered my creativity.

I looked around the room and saw other people thriving—and that's when it dawned on me: being an empathic problem solver takes many forms. There isn't just one way to do it. There are probably loads of ways we can develop understanding. Perhaps my problem wasn't one of inability but one of flexibility.

I flashed back to my first personality-type test in high school. It was the famous Myers-Briggs Type Indicator, and it opened so many layers of understanding about who I was and how I was wired internally. As I sat in the brainstorm, I wondered if people approach things empathically in multiple ways. The idea was too exciting to ignore, and I leapt from my seat and rushed out of the room to begin outlining the idea.

I found myself scribbling notes whenever I observed different ways that others on our team and I were being empathic. Some people couldn't resist asking "Why?" until they got to the heart of a problem. That approach, popularized by Sakichi Toyoda of the Toyota Motor Company, has become known as the "5 Whys." It is based on the belief that after asking "Why?" five times, you can get to the root of what's happening. That was Toyoda's way of being empathic, of seeking to understand a person or problem in its most essential state.

Another colleague was great at creating and holding space. She spent time before a meeting organizing and orienting a host of objects within a room so that everything was designed to elicit the best possible experience for the participants. She knew that some people would want snacks; others liked a little music; and others liked to load up on caffeine. She cued the music and poured the coffee before anyone else arrived. When you walked into a meeting with her, you could immediately drop into a state of comfort, and she had a much easier time getting the team to work with her toward a viable solution.

These and plenty of other examples started to give shape to the empathic archetypes and behaviors at play within our company. But as they became more defined, we realized something profound: no individual operates solely from one archetype. We all have within us a distinct set of work styles, though we are stronger in some and weaker in others. I like to be methodological and linear in my thinking, but that's not the *only* way I know how to solve a problem. I can still call on other styles within me when I need them for those rapid-fire idea sessions I dread so much. I might not love doing so, and I might not be the best at it, but I can do it. It's within me. The more we explored that notion, the more we saw a fuller spectrum of empathy come into focus.

I've also learned to marvel at others who thrive and are productive in situations where I am more challenged. This is all part of experiencing empathy at such moments and learning by observing other work styles. I've even taught myself to improve my own dexterity in styles where I'm less comfortable. By "limbering up" or sharpening those behaviors, I have become a better collaborator with a wider array of people.

LIMBERING UP

If we can "limber up" mentally, we will be able to improve a whole host of things. As creative thinkers, it will give us more flexibility to work in different ways. As managers, it will help us better understand and connect with our team members and provide them the sort of personalized mentorship they need for their growth. And as leaders, it will give us the confidence and sense of nuance necessary to undertake increasingly complex problems for some of the world's biggest companies.

At that point, we were a few months into developing our point of view on empathy, and we were ready to put our thinking into action. We had already begun talking about empathy with our clients, testing to see if it was something they felt was needed in their own companies. Happily, we found that clients from every sector were grappling with the same challenges:

- How could they better understand their customers?
- How could they build an internal culture befitting the individuals on their team?
- Which products or services were they developing that would align with the ever-evolving marketplace?

Those questions and others like them begged to be solved with empathy.

It occurred to us that we were essentially running an ethnographic study of empathy. We were looking for places where it was showing up in business, in culture, in the news. We started an archive into which we gathered as much literature and conversation on the topic as we could find. Brené Brown's work on the subject stands out for me as particularly intriguing—not just because of her elegant and clear-minded thinking and presentations on the topic but also because her online videos were garnering millions of views in amazingly short periods of time. The sheer virality of all this, coupled with the news alerts coming in daily to all of our RSS feeds, showed us that the keyword *empathy* was on the rise in the zeitgeist and being covered in publications as diverse as *Wired*, *Harvard Business Review*, *Sports Illustrated*, and *National Geographic*.

At the same time, we were witnessing a significant shift in the human resources side of many of our corporate clients. No longer were companies interested in people who exhibited only subject-matter expertise. The trend was shifting dramatically toward a hybrid skill set that was first defined by the management consultancy McKinsey & Company in the 1980s and was now experiencing a resurgence. "T-shaped" people—as they are called—are depicted with the "T's" vertical line representing a person's depth in a single expertise, the horizontal line his or her ability to operate broadly across disciplines. A good example of this is a doctor whose specialty might be in infectious diseases but who operates as a general practitioner. Leaders in many different industries were saying that most, if not all, workers in the twenty-first century need to have some sort of "T-shaped" profile if they expect to be competitive in the job market of the future.

We are all born with a vast, three-dimensional dexterity. Your raw skills are a core part of your ability to do your job well, but perhaps the concept "T-shaped" is selling all of us a bit short. After all, where does our ability to be empathic, persuasive, or compassionate fit into the "T"? The real limiting factor on realizing our fullest potential is often the strictures of our professional roles. Jobs with specific functions that require us to work within guardrails can limit our ability to bring forward everything we have to offer. Many people work in organizations that still have outdated hierarchies and processes.

Today's most effective companies are flatter, more collaborative, and more dynamic than ever before. They know how to "fail fast," to "move at the pace of culture," and to do all the other buzzy phrases that fill our office corridors. But buzz phrase or not, companies that behave this way open the door to being more empathic, making themselves more able to understand the world around them and the people who work within their walls. Leaders of such companies get more out of their teams because they recognize that this kind of dexterity is an essential part of our modern work style.

Armed with this realization and a newly minted articulation of our empathic methodology, it was time for us to find a way to help ourselves, and our clients, break away from old conventions while achieving their growth goals and delivering inspiring work to the world. Their outmoded corporate structures and behaviors were like big boulders, and we needed a pretty big fulcrum to move them away. Empathy is that fulcrum. With empathy, complex problems become more understandable, teams become more effective, and companies become more nimble. A key part of sharing this thinking with our clients is done through something we came to call our Empathic Archetypes.

THE ARCHETYPES CRYSTALLIZE

Our goal was to create a set of archetypes people could identify with and use to help them pinpoint their own empathic strengths and shortcomings. We all have our own preferences and cognitive biases, our "default" modes of thinking, feeling, and being. These preferred modes often limit our ability to go beyond our norms and expand our perspectives. The archetypes help shake us out of old patterns and guide us toward new, exciting paths. Through their application, we hope we can cultivate a more deft style of thinking that leads to solutions that are more insightful and well rounded.

We designed the seven Empathic Archetypes as personas that an individual can slip into and use as a way of getting out of his or her own head, role, or organizational hierarchy. Even during the process of creating the archetypes, they began to lead us toward new perspectives and greater understanding.

Before we dive into what the archetypes are, it bears mentioning that I've always been drawn to the mystical. The iconography, language, and symbols of ancient texts have been a fascination of mine for as long as I can remember. These elements even influenced the creation of the Sub Rosa brand. The logo subtly forms a triangle—a key symbol of sacred geometry evoking stability. Even the phrase *sub rosa* is a Latin term used to denote confidentiality. To speak "sub rosa" means you are speaking to someone you can entrust with your secrets. That captured the spirit of what we wanted in our client relationships. We wanted people to know they could come to us with their concerns and challenges. Those were the kinds of topics we wanted to tackle. I wanted clients to know it was safe to share their most important issues with us— things they needed a trusted partner to understand and keep in strict confidence.

Whether clients knew this about us or not, it was important for me to imbue the company with this sensibility and to build upon its ancient foundation. I wanted the archetypes to have the same association with antiquity while also being firmly rooted in what it is like to live and work in the modern world. We wanted words and imagery that would inspire a reverence for the past as much as they provoked and inspired people to move forward.

Our early inspiration for the archetypes' design was found in the tarot. A deck of tarot cards contains an extraordinary fount of fantastic imagery and nuanced symbolism. The cards help people draw on infrequently accessed parts of the psyche as a way of bringing forth new understanding. In a tarot reading, the symbols on the cards are used to offer insights, and it is believed that, intuitively, the "right" cards will be drawn for the situation at hand. Some call these patterns and associations random, others destiny, but whether you think tarot cards are powerful mystic tools or occult hooey, their complex symbology is powerful and born from an artistry that inspired us to develop a set of cards that we could use to provoke new thoughts and challenge existing biases.

A typical tarot deck is divided into two sets of cards called the major and minor arcana. The minor arcana—fifty-six numbered cards divided among four suits—resembles a normal deck of playing cards inasmuch as each suit has a theme and the cards in it have certain hierarchies or numerical order. The major arcana consist of archetypal figures such as the Fool, the Empress, the Magician, and nineteen others. In a reading, these cards and their rich symbolism are used as guides for thinking differently about a problem.

We narrowed our empathic archetypes to seven, and each one was crafted to elevate and celebrate ancestral and sacred practices for understanding the psyche, creating deeper connections, and practicing self-discovery. These archetypes are not gimmicks; their iconography is as old as time. They come to life through their behaviors. An archetype and its behavior represent a way of being that can be applied to almost any task. We now use the seven empathic archetypes to govern the way we work and collaborate.

Think about your own workplace. You undoubtedly have colleagues with vastly different styles of working and collaborating. This is true in every organization. When we were deciding on the archetypes, we intentionally wanted them to represent not only the different behaviors an individual can exhibit but also behaviors that can be expressed between two people who are working together on a project.

The personas are an innate part of all of us—each one tremendously powerful, though distributed within us unequally. We often have different "individuals" within our own psyches, and they vie for attention and control during each situation we face. The archetypes are a way of putting a name to the behaviors most commonly called upon when we are attempting to act with empathy. We all have different comfort levels with the archetypes. Some fit with us naturally, while others can feel entirely foreign.

At the functional core of each archetype, both emotional intelligence and self-observation are at play, reinforcing the importance of emotions and actions and revealing our own strengths and limits, as well as the perspectives of others, always reminding us to take an active interest in ourselves and in other people.

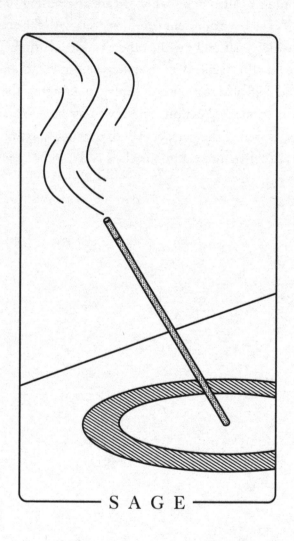

SAGE

SEVEN EMPATHIC PERSONAS, SEVEN ARCHETYPES

1. The Sage
Be present: Inhabit the here and now.

We discovered the Sage during our work with GE when we realized that deep insight can emerge when we are fully present in a space together. During this project, we had a few ground rules that helped us to remain fully present in our SoHo space: no phones, no computers, no cross talk. Those simple behaviors led our team members to be respectful, contemplative, and fully in the moment with one another. We saw how those simple behavioral adjustments created an environment in which deeper understanding could be attained.

The Sage represents wisdom and the ability to be fully in the moment, sensing truths about the mind, body, and surrounding space, examining what is brought into the moment and what is meant to be taken away. Look to the Sage when a situation becomes untethered from the present and disconnected from reality. Relying on this archetype will help you bring people and their ideas back to the here and now.

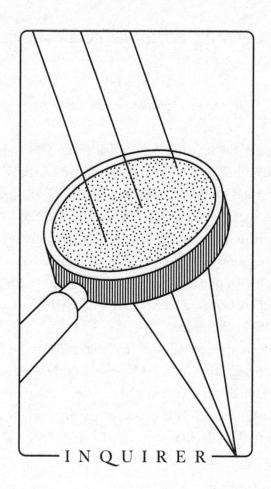

INQUIRER

2. The Inquirer

Question: Interrogate assumed truths.

The Inquirers on our team have strengths that harken back to the lessons of the "5 Whys." They are deeply curious question askers who don't stop at the first response but probe deeper, looking for more complete understanding. We saw this emerge in the mammography assignment when we began asking why the examination rooms were so cold. By asking this over and over, going deeper down the rabbit hole, we eventually reached an opportunity for improvement that was a key to our success.

The Inquirer is one part reporter, another part therapist. This archetype challenges preconceived notions and pushes for deeper, more authentic truths. Inquirers neglect small talk in favor of "big" talk: deep questions that demand contemplative responses. Always intrigued by the "why" behind each answer, Inquirers dig and dig until they reach the root.

CONVENER

3. The Convener

Host: Anticipate the needs of others.

So much of the overall experience we created in SoHo was a result of this archetype. The Conveners on our team knew that establishing a sense of community would bring out the truth from everyone with whom we interacted. Everything from the furnishings to the food and drink was selected to inspire a sense of safety, security, and comfort. That provided all of our participants the comfort they needed so they could drop into deep conversation quickly. From that we got loads of information—both verbally and nonverbally—that helped us design a better overall patient experience.

The consummate host, the Convener understands the importance of space and space holding. Recognizing that every detail is critical, the Convener creates a purposeful, appropriate setting for the work at hand. The space we share is an active member of the experience. The Convener anticipates what you need before you do and brings the space surrounding you to life.

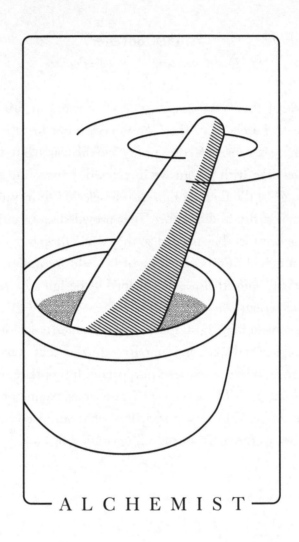

A L C H E M I S T

4. The Alchemist

Experiment: Test and learn at all costs.

The Alchemist emerged when we built waiting rooms and prototype exam rooms. They were spaces where we were able to experiment and test different ways in which women experience a mammogram. Such behavior is prevalent in many of the projects we analyzed in developing the archetypes and is a powerful tool often used in many innovation and design firms. The willingness to test and learn is an empathic behavior that delivers powerful understanding and impactful solutions.

Never afraid to fail in the pursuit of knowledge, the Alchemist tests everything, confident that the best work comes only from countless hours of experimentation. The Alchemist is curious, persistent, and patient, takes a chance on a new approach, and closely studies the results. Turn to the Alchemist when the only path to a solution lies through the brambles of resistance.

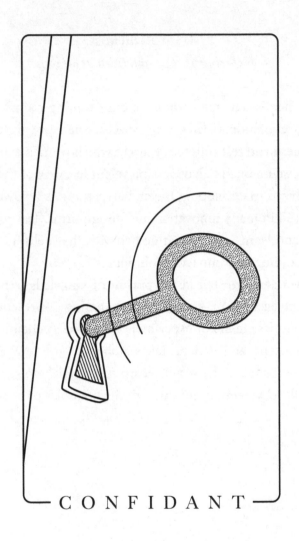

C O N F I D A N T

5. The Confidant

Listen: Develop the ability to observe and absorb.

Creating a sense of confidence is paramount to the work we do. For GE, we knew that once we created a private, safe environment, the participants would become more open about describing the fears and anxieties involved in the mammography experience. We had the space covered by the Convener, but we needed to show up in the space and listen. Our team brought a sense of patience and a willingness to open up to each participant. We listened fully and absorbed every ounce of information the women shared with us. In many ways, this is a strategist's first and primary skill: to shut off the inner dialogue and purely listen. Over time, I began to see how the Confidant was showing up not only on this project but on many others as well.

Your trusted ally, the Confidant hears to listen—instead of simultaneously planning what to say next. The Confidant embodies stillness; listens, observes, and absorbs. Keeping what you hear safe on behalf of another is what gives them a sense of integrity and strength. Look to the Confidant when asked for advice or when others need to share something of importance. The Confidant provides emotional security and comfort.

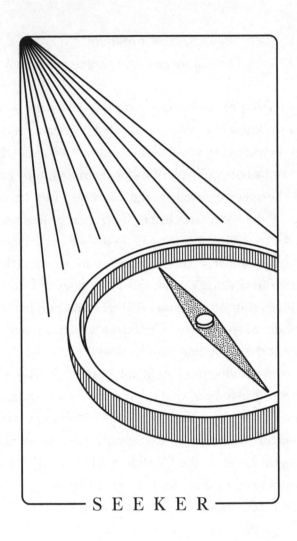

SEEKER

6. The Seeker

Dare: Be confident and fearless.

Seekers are daring. They are confident and fearless. Frankly, if we hadn't had a bit of the Seeker running within us, we probably couldn't have undertaken the mammography project at all. The Seeker gave us the assuredness we needed to take on such a daunting challenge and be unafraid to do things differently. I have discovered in my own self-work that I often operate from this archetype. Entrepreneurs are inherent risk-takers, and they must dare in order to be successful.

A boundless explorer, the Seeker bravely sets out on new adventures. The Seeker lives outside his or her comfort zone, acts with confidence and self-assurance. Embody the Seeker when embracing new experiences and daunting challenges, knowing that unfettering your pursuits will eventually lead you to the answer.

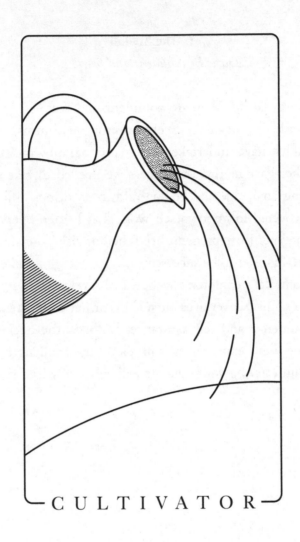

CULTIVATOR

7. The Cultivator

Commit: Nurture with purpose and intentionally grow.

Cultivators have powerful vision. They understand that we commit to things today as a way of getting what we want in the future. Most people get so caught up in the day-to-day that they lose sight of the long game. The Cultivator remembers to maintain a state of empathy for the point he or she is working toward, even if it's far out on the horizon. In our work with GE, we constantly reminded our team that the work we were doing was bigger than selling more machinery. It was about improving the overall patient experience and potentially having an impact on the lives of those involved.

The Cultivator is committed to developing ideas and is intentional about every action. Through the Cultivator, you can connect everything you do to the development and maintenance of your thoughts and work. When something feels daunting and protracted, look to the Cultivator to provide perspective and leadership. Naturally gifted at seeing the greater purpose, the Cultivator knows what it takes to reap what he or she has sown.

CHAPTER TWO EXERCISES

Archetype Exemplars

We can now begin to build a deeper familiarity with the seven Empathic Archetypes. A method we've found helpful is to think about someone in your life or the world who personifies each archetype the most. Think of this exercise as discovering your archetype exemplars.

To some, the Convener, whose behavior is to host, immediately brings to mind Martha Stewart or other well-known lifestyle gurus. Others might imagine a maître d' at their favorite restaurant or their yoga instructor. Each of these perfectly embodies the spirit of the Convener.

Assign to each archetype a real-life person who embodies its behavior. Doing so will help bring the archetypes alive for you and will bring them closer to your own reality. It will also help you understand and work with the archetypes more readily.

Self-Assessment and Application

Once you have a better understanding of the archetypes, it's time to connect with your personal strengths and weaknesses. You must be honest with yourself about this work. No one is evenly distributed across all seven archetypes; a good way to determine where you index on each of them is to personalize them.

Personalizing the Archetypes

Reread each of the archetypes, keeping in mind the real-life exemplars you have assigned to each one. Now, for each archetype, look back on your own life and identify a moment in your past where you clearly embodied the archetype fully. Remember how it felt when you were in that moment. Were you happy? Anxious? At ease?

As you do this exercise, journal your memories of these experiences. Consider how easy or hard it was for you to find an example in your past. Did it come to you immediately, or was it difficult to find one? How did you feel in those moments? Was the feeling natural or unnatural? These are the clues that will help you to understand your strengths and weaknesses across all seven archetypes.

Use the spider graph on the next page, or one you sketch yourself, to plot where you felt most to least comfortable with each archetype, and a clear picture will start to emerge.

With this assessment of where you stand with the strengths and weaknesses of each archetype, you can begin "trying on" each one. One of the ways I try to improve my ability to shift among archetypes with greater ease is by pushing myself to work through the ones that make me the most uncomfortable. You can also identify specific ways you can "show up" in the perspective of a particular archetype and make them part of your daily practice.

For example, let's look at the Alchemist, whose behavior is testing and learning, experimentation at all costs. Ask yourself each day how you can challenge yourself to experiment. It doesn't have to be huge. You don't need to dive into particle physics. Perhaps you have always been intimidated by cooking. Now is your chance to pick up some groceries and make something for yourself. You will probably not like the feeling of being outside of your comfort zone, but stick with it.

See how you look at problems from this perspective. How do you grapple with not knowing how the dish will turn out while you're prepping the ingredients? Does it make you anxious? Those who thrive in this archetype become exhilarated at this moment of experimentation. See if you can find a way to experience the joy that comes from this experimentation. Over time, you'll discover how the mind of an Alchemist works and the sort of state you can embody in order to connect with it more fully. Do the same for each archetype in order to understand your strengths and weaknesses better.

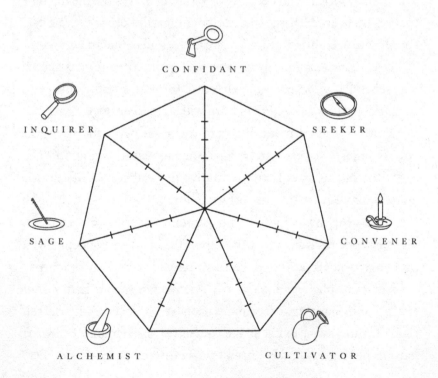

CONFIDANT

INQUIRER

SEEKER

SAGE

CONVENER

ALCHEMIST

CULTIVATOR

Connecting to Your Whole Self

In college, I thought management consulting—providing solutions to companies and helping them think through complex problems—sounded incredibly interesting, and I was sure that was what I wanted to do. I even imagined what it would be like working at one of the big shops such as Bain, or Booz Allen Hamilton, or Deloitte. It seemed like the kind of thing I would enjoy.

But as the saying goes, "Man plans and God laughs."

My path has taken me in a different direction, but the thing I've held on to from those dreamy undergrad days is that deep down I knew I wanted to solve cerebral, intricate problems. What I would come to find as Sub Rosa grew was that we're able to do something special that consultants rarely get the chance to experience: we actually get to enact the solutions we recommend. We're not just recommenders, we're doers. Many of our clients have told me stories about hiring consultants who work with them for months to develop a big new strategy. They research and do the analysis they need in order to finally deliver a massive, often complex document that drops with a thud onto the client's conference room table. It's a perfectly crafted panacea for all that ails the client.

But too often the solutions the consultants produce are disconnected from the implementation. They haven't been crafted by implementers, and as a result, they sometimes miss the key elements needed to bring the strategy or solution to life. In a word, the consultants lack empathy. Though I didn't know it back in my college days, the connection between thinking and doing, between recommending and acting—that is what real empathic problem-solving requires.

At Sub Rosa, my colleagues and I often have the opportunity to engage with clients from start to finish. When we have clients who want to work with us in this way, the process is much more holistic. They understand the high degree of interconnectedness between the two types of work, and they value a partner who can work alongside them to bring well-rounded solutions to life. These are the best kind of clients.

Nike is one of them.

One day, Nike came knocking on our door with a visionary new product it was introducing, and it needed our help to solve a strategic and executional challenge. The company wasn't just looking for a clever marketing idea; it was looking for a partner who could work with its product, marketing, and communication teams to build a strategy to introduce a new shoe with special technical features to the general market in a way that would tout its innovative properties while also being understandable. It was right up our alley.

Sub Rosa had already done several assignments for Nike—projects that had experimented with and challenged convention. We'd put together artist collaborations that commissioned diverse forms of installation art with new materials being introduced by Nike. We'd designed exclusive, ultrapremium retail lounges where high-end customers could create bespoke sneakers in a private suite alongside a Nike designer. We had established such a trusting relationship while working together that when Nike needed to do something disruptive, we were sometimes fortunate enough to receive the call.

By 2013, Nike had been working on this product for several years, and it was something the market had never seen. Some of Nike's best and brightest manufacturing and material technology came together to create the Nike Free Hyperfeel.

Nike has an amazing lab called "the Kitchen," where researchers and designers study performance, materials, the physiology of elite athletes, and a whole host of other things that help Nike continue to be a cutting-edge powerhouse. In the many years we've worked together, I've been inside the Kitchen only once, and it was like being inside Willy Wonka's factory. Only it smelled a lot more like fresh rubber than chocolate.

After countless tests in the Kitchen, the Nike team arrived at the Nike Free Hyperfeel—a new running shoe that is ultrasensorial, form-fitting, and higher performance than ever before. The shoe combined some of Nike's already existing technologies, such as Flyknit (a weaving technology that uses high-performance fabric to sew the top of the shoe, replacing the less ecological and more costly leather, stitching, and gluing process), as well as a Lunarlon insole, which molds more naturally to the bottom of the foot, and Dynamic Flywire, which allows the shoe to flex and contract like ligaments in the body.

It was a big deal.

Hyperfeel represented years of research and development, and the story was a tricky one to communicate. There were tons of attributes—the material science, the design, the research that had led to the product's creation—that needed to be woven together to launch the product successfully. Nike wanted to have people hear about the technology that had gone into it, to be impressed by it, and to actually *feel* it.

We needed to create an experience that would wow consumers not only with how the shoe looked but also with how it felt on their feet—and we knew that empathy held the key to solving this. We turned to the Seven Archetypes to help our team gain the broadest, most empathic understanding of what we wanted to communicate. But early on I realized that if we wanted to apply empathy to this particular problem, we would need to go deeper in order to engage with consumers on multiple levels. It led us to the creation of something we refer to as the Whole Self—a philosophy largely inspired by my meetings with a man named Gil Barretto, an intellectual and spiritual "athlete" of Olympic proportions.

OPENING DOORS LEFT-HANDED

His voice had a subtle booming quality. He didn't yell. He didn't even speak loudly. But his tone had a gravitas and a rumble that made his words land on my ears in a way that made me uncomfortable yet inspired me at the same time.

"How present are you?" he asked matter-of-factly.

I was twenty-eight years old at the time and thought I knew everything there was to know about life. I was switched on. I was insightful. I was definitely present. And I was sure I relayed as much as I attempted to summon a sense of humility through my young and oblivious pride.

Gil smiled back and asked a simple question: "Are you right-handed?"

"Yes," I responded.

"Good. Here's what I'd like you to do. . . . When you leave here today, I want you to open every door you approach with your left hand."

I thought to myself, *That's it? Easy enough.*

That was one of my early visits to Gil Barretto, a man who would become a mentor and a guide and who would play an intimate role in my personal and spiritual development for the seven years we worked together before his passing. I met Gil through a series of fortuitous circumstances. For a few years, I had been part of a monthly meditation group hosted by my dear friend Alexandra. Alex is a kind and mystical woman who is about ten years my senior. She'd been working on her own mindfulness for a long while and had opened her door to help others seeking a more present way of being. We'd spend time each month talking about the work of G. I. Gurdjieff and Carl Jung, the finer points of the Nag Hammadi Library, and other esoteric works. It was a powerful time for me that opened my eyes and my spirit to a world much bigger than myself.

One day Alex said she thought it was time I connected with Gil. She had referred to Gil from time to time in passing. She'd say something about how she and Gil were talking about such and such or that she'd be seeing him at a monthly gathering of his students. I didn't know what Gil taught or what being his student entailed, but I was intrigued. When she offered to introduce us, I happily agreed.

After my first session with Gil, I spent the next week opening countless doors, only to realize on the other side that my right hand was recoiling from the handle and returning to my side. "I did it again," I'd tell myself. It was beyond frustrating.

I couldn't believe that something as simple as opening a door with my nondominant hand could be so difficult. But I wasn't in the moment. I was unconsciously moving through life while my mind continued to race through an inner monologue at a million miles an hour.

Of Gil's many gifts, his ability to help others see this about themselves was one of his best. He knew how to assign a simple action, something that would require presence and discipline and that, if adhered to over time, would lead to a heightened sense of self-awareness. That's what the doorknob assignment did. It made me realize that I was rarely, if ever, actually present. To put it another way, I had no empathy for myself. I was completely detached and had no real understanding of who I was or where I was.

I was always thinking about something else. Where I was going. The meeting I had just left. What I wanted for dinner. Anything other than the present moment—or even the door in front of me and the conscious act of opening it with my left hand.

Gil looked like a Navajo elder, though actually he was mostly Puerto Rican, hailing from Spanish Harlem. If you looked at him long enough, he'd start to look like any number of ethnicities. He was timeless and raceless, and though he was entirely self-aware, he was selfless, caring for his students as they fought their inner battles. He never missed a meeting or started late. He was in his late seventies when I met him, but he still stood over six feet tall and had broad shoulders. He always wore a shirt and tie and expected the same of me when we met about three times a month.

He'd lived in India with gurus, he'd studied beside esoteric scholars in far-flung corners of the world, and he'd trained with descendants from the twentieth-century spiritual teacher G. I. Gurdjieff's school. He had been educated as a psychologist, and he played a mean saxophone. He didn't have a particular philosophy that he preached. He wasn't interested in filling his students with his own dogma. He once said that if my god was an umbrella, his job was to help me understand and believe in that umbrella better than ever before. His own experiences and study had given him powerful tools to help his students on the road to self-understanding. That was what made Gil so special.

I kept trying to master the door-opening exercise and would return to Gil time after time, lamenting that I wasn't getting it. Eventually, after about four months of work, I was able to pro-claim my success. "I'm doing it, Gil!"

He smiled a half-grin and said, "Good. Now switch back."

It took me a few more months of the exercise before I began to figure out what it was really about. I had begun to breathe more slowly. I was in my body. I was becoming more present. I was learning how to quiet the inner dialogue that had me run-ning around like a madman. I was beginning to understand my inner self.

That was what Gil had been striving for all along. He was dis-mantling some of my bad internal habits. He was helping me to see the different "I's" that were driving my actions. Some days it was a manic "I" who couldn't stop thinking about work and clients and managing the growing complexity of the company. Other "I's" were self-destructive, self-indulgent, or simply lazy. I got to know all of them and was able to see that each of them was a lesser ver-sion of the man I wanted to become. The nearly constant state of self-observation Gil had put me into had helped me notice when the wrong "I" was showing up and trying to run the show.

So in a way, Gil saved my life. He didn't pull me from a burn-ing building or take a bullet for me, but he might as well have. He stepped in front of a false version of myself that was at the wheel of my mind and body. He spotted in me a more essential, more capable "I" and over time, with additional training and dialogue, he helped me regain control of a self that was careening toward disaster.

Sometimes a session with Gil seemed like talk therapy. I'd go on and on about what was happening in my daily life, and he would let me talk as his silent gaze looked into something deeper. After I had rambled on for probably thirty minutes, he'd usually ask a sharp and powerful question such as "Why do you think I should care about any of this?" or "Who's talking right now?" Those questions would knock me back and make me rethink everything I'd just said.

Other times we sat across from each other, gazing into each other's eyes for a long period of time. The room would seem to change dramatically. The light would shift. Even Gil's face would start to change. In those moments I'd see or sense something, some sort of information lying just beyond my normal perception. Gil knew how to help me access that information; to see and hear it in a way that was understandable, while also crazy and entirely mystical. Powerful things would happen in his office. I never quite knew what to expect, and even when we had a tough session that left me in tears, I never regretted our meetings.

During the time I worked with Gil, I began to know myself more fully, and I came to refine my own philosophies on personal development and, more specifically, on empathy. It's been about a decade since we first met, and Gil passed away a few years ago—peacefully and in his own way—but he still walks with me every day.

After Gil's passing, I began to think more and more about empathy and what it really meant. I thought about how most of us spend so much time trying to get a grasp on one another, but rarely do we take the time to delve deep and try to understand our own selves.

THE WHOLE SELF

Philosophers and psychologists have suggested for years that each of us is made up of many "selves." Carl Jung referred to them as opposing attitudes of the ego and the unconscious. William James is quoted as saying, "Properly speaking, a man has as many social selves as there are individuals who recognize him." Emmanuel Kant wrote extensively about the "I of reflection" that we encounter through apperception. This stuff can get really heady, really fast.

I've taken bits of philosophy that have resonated with me and tried them on for size. Some fit nicely, others were cumbersome and clunky. Over time, I've come to believe that we have within us seven distinct facets of self. When they are working together, aligned and empowered, we understand ourselves fully. When they are in discord, imbalanced and confused, we cannot become the leaders, creators, or partners we want to be.

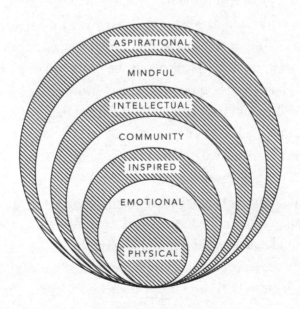

These seven selves begin at our roots. The first to consider is the **Physical Self,** which helps us explore the power of our presence and experience the environment around us. Gil's early lesson with the doorknobs was engaging me in a kind of kinesthetic learning in which I was becoming more aware of myself through action and movement. He was pushing me to get into touch with my physical presence, to inhabit the here and now, and to be in command of my own body. Without this sort of presence, any other more cerebral pursuits are futile.

Next is our **Emotional Self,** which connects us to our personal needs and our inner voice, giving us a means to achieve greater understanding and self-knowledge. This self helps us understand our biases, our fears, and our self-imposed limitations and constrictions. Talk therapy is a great way to explore this realm of the self. This therapy is often diagnostic, and ideally, when effective, it can lead to actionable behavioral changes that help us come into our true "self."

The **Inspired Self** is the spark that ignites the inherent desire to make, to do, and to solve. We engage with this self when we establish goals or intentions we want to pursue and then take the steps to act upon them. Think about the times you've set a goal for yourself, then acted upon it and accomplished it. The deep sense of accomplishment you get fuels the Inspired Self and encourages us to set new goals.

Unfortunately, many of us get stuck in this self, especially those of us in the business world who thrive on the achievement of measured goals, to the exclusion of the other aspects of the self, causing us to hold ourselves back from a deeper, more whole sense of understanding and personal growth.

Having grasped our physical, emotional, and inspired states of being, we can begin to look at how we fit within the context of the world around us. What role do we play among our family, friends, and colleagues? This is the **Community Self**, and it helps us understand how our individual self interacts with the world around us. What type of person are we at work? At home? Do people rely on us the same way? Do we provide different things to different people, or are our core aspects of ourselves relied upon in a similar way irrespective of the people around us? The Community Self helps us know what others most often rely upon us to do and helps us contextualize the "fit" of our relationships.

If people ask us to behave in a manner consistent with our own views and the intent of our Whole Self, we can work with others effectively. But when we are urged to deviate from our authentic self, to act in ways that pull us from our core beliefs, it is often an indicator that we need to do some personal work to improve our sense of agency or the dynamics of our relationships.

One way we can make such changes is to begin to engage with the **Intellectual Self.** This is the self that asks questions both old and new, micro and macro, universal and specific, to help us get a grasp on our perspective and communicate it effectively. At times our emotions are complex and hard to manage. How many times have you acted out of anger and said something you shouldn't have? Or been so overjoyed that you saw a situation through rose-colored glasses, obscuring the reality? The Intellectual Self helps put our emotions and senses into concepts and words that help us understand what's going on inside us and relate more effectively to those around us.

Mindfulness is an ancient topic that has become increasingly popular again. The growing interest in meditation, from tried-and-true forms such as Vedic and Zen meditation to more contemporary modalities such as Transcendental Meditation (TM) and facilitation tools such as the popular app Headspace, have helped people the world over to become more conscious and aware. It's no coincidence that in these trying times, we are seeing more people, of all demographics and psychographics, begin to explore a more mindful state of being. This is the nature of the **Mindful Self.** This self's primary function is to raise our consciousness for the present moment, our relationship with the world around us in this moment, and our place in it.

Once we had outlined these six selves—the Physical, Emotional, Inspired, Community, Intellectual, and Mindful—I thought about what these different facets of our inner workings add up to. What kind of clarity do they create?

For me, they come together in an awareness of our **Aspirational Self.** Some might call this our purpose. This is what we strive for and constantly pursue. It clarifies the vision we have of our growth and what we see as the necessary steps to getting us there.

It is in our nature to grow, to learn lessons, and to evolve. Many great spiritual teachers, spanning all religions and sects, have shared this lesson with us for millennia. The pursuit and acceptance of the Aspirational Self allows our lives to gain meaning. Having a sense of our greater purpose is like the magnetism that keeps a compass needle pointing toward the north. With clarity of purpose, we can make choices and take actions clear-mindedly.

These are the aspects of the Whole Self.

It is no coincidence that they correspond with many ancient teachings. Those who are familiar with the Eastern concept of the chakras can see how these seven facets of the Whole Self correspond with the seven primary chakras. They, like other mind/body mapping frameworks such as the Chinese dantians, are used to help translate ancient wisdom into understandable states of knowledge.

Though I have invested countless hours into thinking deeply about these matters, exploring my own personal development, and relaying my thoughts to others who are walking along a similar path, I do not believe there is a finish line because these pursuits are never fully finished. Instead, maintaining an awareness of the Whole Self is a constant practice of self-attention and awareness, affording us the opportunity to notice when we are losing track of a part of our self and enabling us to make small course corrections or adjustments to regain alignment.

Do I still open doors unconsciously from time to time? Absolutely. But I also know that through the daily, hourly, and moment-to-moment act of self-observation, we can understand and attain a better and more whole self.

Even if just for a moment.

THE ART AND SCIENCE OF FEELING

At Nike, a pair of size 13s was waiting for me. Wearing a pair of Nike Hyperfeels felt like wearing a padded sock. That was the first thought I had when I slipped my feet into the stretchy material. When I walked, I could feel the texture of the concrete below my feet. It was weird. I wasn't barefoot, but the shoes made me feel something close to barefoot.

Others from our team had a similar experience. We began to talk more about going barefoot and how rarely any of us was outside our apartments without shoes on. (I mean, after all, we do live in New York, and who knows what might be lurking on the sidewalks waiting to jab, cut, or poke our feet.) The Nike Hyperfeel was built on more than ten years of learning from the company's Nike Free franchise, which they had launched in 2005. Nike Free was grounded on the notion that barefoot running strengthens your feet. As our Sub Rosa team did its research for Hyperfeel, we talked to runners who said they knew about the growing "barefoot running" trend and the fact that many athletes had started running without shoes as part of their training.

A number of them told us that the most notable moment for barefoot running happened at the starting line of the Summer Olympics marathon in Rome more than fifty years earlier. Abebe Bikila, an unknown Ethiopian marathoner, lined up barefoot next to some of the world's top runners. A little more than two hours later, he was the first to cross the finish line, his bare feet leaving a trail of runners behind him.

Since then, the trend has continued to ebb and flow in popular culture. In 2009, the book *Born to Run*, which was in part about barefoot running, was released and sold millions of copies. This added to the frenzy already started by the Nike Free shoes, and led to an emergence in barefoot running. The more we researched the subject, the more information we discovered. Barefoot running helps change the way your foot strikes the ground. You become more aware of your gait, and some runners even say you can reach a more meditative state while running barefoot. We knew that if we could elucidate the power of this mind-body connection, we could show how Nike's new product would help people fully connect with their feet, themselves, and the world around them.

We looked at the seven aspects of the Whole Self and applied each one to the feet and the experience of running; and then we considered how we could integrate those insights with the whole body and mind. Soon an outline for our strategy began to form.

- *The Physical Self:* We would use the feet as part of the overall product launch.
- *The Emotional Self:* We would find a way to heighten the emotional response to the activity of placing the feet on the ground (or floor).
- *The Inspired Self:* We would create an experience that would prompt participants to want to learn more about the barefoot running trend.
- *The Community Self:* We would design the experience in a way that would compel the participants to connect with one another about what had happened to them.
- *The Intellectual Self:* We would provoke a sense of curiosity in the participants by communicating information to them in a nontraditional and sensorial way.
- *The Mindful Self:* We would encourage the participants to reach a state of connection to the present moment and the world around them through an immersive experience.
- *The Aspirational Self:* We would give the participants a takeaway that would reveal something about themselves they didn't already know, which they could use in the pursuit of their higher goals.

At least, that was the plan. We still needed to come up with the big idea, but those were definitely our building blocks. We knew that connecting with some of these selves would be more difficult than others, but considering the effect the shoes had had on us, it made sense to incorporate the concept of the Whole Self.

We started to think about how we could use Hyperfeel to get people more engaged in the act of running. We talked about having a group run in the shoes, followed by a workshop in which the participants would give us feedback. Those ideas were okay but didn't really tick all the boxes.

Then it hit us. We wanted to have people really connect with the value of the Nike Free Hyperfeel, and to do that, we needed to have them appreciate the experience of being barefoot. Most people haven't run barefoot, and many just slip on a pair of socks, regular running shoes, and go. They don't feel the ground, and they don't have the sensorial connection to what's below them. We needed to change that if we were to contribute to the successful launch of the Hyperfeel. We had to lead people to empathy for the experience of being barefoot.

PLEASE TAKE OFF YOUR SHOES AND SOCKS

We wanted to create a sensorial experience that would allow people to engage with the soles of their feet, recognizing the role they play as sense receptors. From there, they would discover for themselves how using their feet in this way can positively influence their own meditative state.

Over the years, we've worked with many different clients. The ones who are the most fun are those who are as thoughtful as they are brave, who are willing to take calculated risks when they believe those risks are in the best interest of the brand and the business. Nike is one of those clients. Our clients quickly greenlit our concept, and before we knew it, we were in preproduction to design and build an immersive 4,000-square-foot labyrinth in the middle of downtown Manhattan.

We designed the Hyperfeel experience to be explored in the dark. From the outside, it was a black-on-black, monolithic-looking structure with a subtle, illuminated Nike swoosh on the side. We provided no explanation about what was happening on the inside. For us, that was part of the intrigue of the experience. The exterior wasn't where the story was being told. What mattered was what people found inside—and ultimately inside themselves.

The guest list was full of important members of the media as well as influencers from the sports community. Olympic runners, professional athletes, and members of local running clubs were all queuing up to experience what was going on inside the mystery box. Such campaigns, ones geared toward influencers, are designed to drive buzz and awareness. By reaching a few thousand influential people and giving them a powerful experience, we were counting on them to spread the story of Hyperfeel and create a word-of-mouth campaign. I always trust news I hear from my friends more than what I hear from advertisements. Our goal was to create believers in the product by doing what we do best: letting them connect empathically with the product and its story. If we got that right, everything else would take care of itself.

Once inside, guests were greeted and asked to take a seat. Next we asked them to take off their shoes and socks. We then attached a smartphone to each person's arm and rigged them with a sensor that would track their brain waves. We let them know we were doing it as a way of capturing data for "something that will be revealed at the end of the experience."

It's difficult enough to get consumers to do experimental stuff, but athletes and members of the media are even more dubious about this sort of marketing. We weren't telling them what was going to happen inside, which made it even more challenging. But we applied empathy in anticipating how they would react to what we were asking them to do, and we let them know that we actually *wanted* them to be skeptical. We didn't want them to be easily convinced. We just hoped they would go into the experience with an open mind and see what happened.

That simple conversation—a subtle but direct addressing of what we empathically knew was a point of resistance—helped us reach a place of trust and collaboration with the participants.

Everyone was up for it.

One by one, we led them through a dark curtain and into the pitch-black labyrinth. They were told that the only way to get to the other side was to trust their feet and feel the textures below them. As the texture of the floor changed, they were encouraged to pause for a moment and stand on the particular material to see how it made them feel. We asked them to use their feet as a guide and keep walking until they found the next texture. They moved from rubber to asphalt, from wet rocks to grass, and on over a variety of other surfaces along the journey.

Our sensors let us know where people were in the maze, and we could trigger audio or lighting effects to guide them if they got lost.

Some people flew through the space and were on the other side in five minutes, but others took their time, enjoying hanging out in the darkness and sensing the space around them. One person spent a little more than thirty minutes inside. A few people on our team debated going in after him, but while they were deciding, he emerged at the exit with a wide smile on his face.

Once the participants reached the end, we removed the sensors and downloaded the brain-wave data we'd collected. We projected the results onto a six-foot circular surface in a sort of abstract digital mandala where they could see their brain-wave activity as they had moved from surface to surface. That gave each participant a unique insight into his or her own neurological experience, and the participants began to realize what powerful sense receptors their feet were.

Some of them learned that their brain was at its most meditative state when they were standing on grass, yet every day they ran on a city street. As more data was revealed, people began having interesting conversations about how they might change their running routes to help put them into a better position to be in a more relaxed, calmer mental state.

That was the point.

Our part in Nike's overall launch of the Hyperfeel was not just to sell a shoe; we wanted to show how this particular product, and the new technology that had gone into it, could lead people to become more fully engaged with the world around them—all through the soles of their feet.

We gave each participant a custom print of his or her mandala, and sent all of them a digital version they could share in social media. Over a three-day period, we hosted more than a thousand people in the space. As they left and shared their experiences online, we were able to launch the shoe to millions of people with real firsthand accounts of what it felt like to wear the new product. The press started to pick up the story, and that played into Nike's overall marketing launch of Hyperfeel, and soon the shoe was part of the national conversation.

The shoes flew off the shelves, and Nike sold out of the first run within days of the launch. It was a huge success.

But for us it was more than a success with a client; it showed that applying empathy, with an emphasis on the Whole Self, was an effective means of solving a problem. We weren't just trying to sell a product; we looked at all facets of the experience and delivered something that truly addressed each component of the whole self—giving people an experience that engaged every part of their being.

The Whole Self in Action

- *The Physical Self:* We made the feet, and particularly their soles, the core input for the overall experience. We focused attention and awareness at the physical body level.
- *The Emotional Self:* By using different textures on the floor, as well as the light and sound triggers, we created external stimuli that gave the participants something that engaged their emotions. They were sometimes confused, sometimes peaceful, and sometimes excited, but all of them said they had run through a range of emotions as they walked through the space.
- *The Inspired Self:* Each participant came away more fully aware of his or her states of awareness and relaxation. Many of them said they were inspired to think about their bodies differently and to consider how small changes in their routines could have an impact on their overall well-being. Many went away with new goals or ambitions for their personal training routines.
- *The Community Self:* Though this was an individual experience, many of the participants stayed after because they wanted to talk with the others, learning from them and feeling more connected with the community of participants. In addition, their willingness to share their experiences with their own net-

works was a testament to how meaningful the journey had been.

- *The Intellectual Self:* Everyone who left the labyrinth was newly aware of how powerful the feet are as sense receptors. They understood Nike's philosophy and technology better, and they could see how the technology could help them understand their own selves better.
- *The Mindful Self:* We engaged with people at a mindful level, and they engaged with themselves. They knew their connection to the space around them more intimately. Their senses were heightened, and their ability to feel the world around them was ultimately enhanced.
- *The Aspirational Self:* In the end, many participants walked away having moved their understanding of themselves a little further down the field. They had learned something meaningful about themselves and were more committed to changing or pushing themselves in a new or different way to more fully experience their mind-body connection.

In pulling it all together, we created an experience that was holistic and all-encompassing, and we also helped the participants connect more fully with themselves and the world around them.

LUCKY NUMBER 7

As we were finishing the Nike Hyperfeel campaign, Gil was very much in my mind, saying with a smile on his face, "Open every door you come to with your left hand, and see what you find."

That simple exercise had taught me how to engage with my whole self, and that had changed me forever.

Years after the Hyperfeel launch, I looked back on the work and the philosophical foundation we had built around empathy. It was clear that the seven Empathic Archetypes and the seven aspects of the Whole Self had something to do with each other. There was no question that the archetypes on their own were helpful, but my team and I were looking for ways to train our empathy. We wanted to really work with the archetypes, and all of a sudden it clicked: we could ask ourselves questions framed by the seven aspects of the Whole Self, and those questions would lead us to probe deeper into each archetype.

A group of us spent weeks thinking through a series of questions that would weave the two concepts together. In the end, each archetype was given a series of seven questions, one for each facet of the Whole Self, and we used those questions to provoke deeper insight and understanding for one another and, ultimately, for ourselves.

Here are the questions we developed for each of the Empathic Archetypes. They are arranged in the descending order of the Whole Self, starting with Aspirational at the top and moving down through Mindful, Intellectual, Community, Inspired, Emotional, and Physical.

The Sage
- What is your purpose?
- Where do you feel most present?
- How has your past shaped who you are?
- What is a lesson you have imparted to others?
- When negative emotions arise, how do you deal with them?

- How do you stay grounded when the world gets overwhelming?
- How do you nurture yourself and your practice?

The Inquirer
- What do you most want to know?
- What personal biases interfere most with your finding truth?
- When have your instincts led you astray?
- Whom do you go to with tough questions?
- What do you continually ask yourself?
- What types of inquiries make you most uncomfortable?
- How does your body communicate?

The Convener
- Where is your favorite place to be a guest?
- How do you balance being self-serving and selfless?
- What makes an experience meaningful?
- Whom do you collaborate with best?
- What are a host's greatest skills?
- What about you most comforts others?
- When do you bring people together?

The Alchemist
- What motivates you to progress?
- What does approaching a breakthrough feel like?
- When does your curiosity create difficulty?
- Who has challenged you to be better than you once were?
- How does iteration inform the outcome of your work?

- What are the biggest sacrifices you've made?
- Where do you go to experiment?

The Confidant

- When is listening more valuable than counseling?
- What role can silence play in a conversation?
- How do you build trust?
- When have you breached a confidence?
- What should people better understand about you?
- How do you protect yourself?
- When are you the most observant?

The Seeker

- What mistake would you make again?
- How do you explore your inner self?
- When is failure productive?
- Who inspires a sense of adventure within you?
- How does courage manifest in your work?
- When does bravery become foolhardy?
- Where do you go to push your limits?

The Cultivator

- What are your most audacious aspirations?
- How do you build endurance?
- What do you purposefully leave undone?
- Who are your long-term partners?
- What commitment have you made to yourself more than once?
- When has mentorship played a role in your life?
- Where do you feel most nurtured?

With those questions completed, we decided it was time to take our thinking to the world. To do so, we created a deck of cards. After all, the tarot had been one of our biggest inspirations for the archetypes. We called the deck "Q&E," which stands for "Questions and Empathy." I use the cards in all sorts of settings, from workshops and client kickoffs to internal projects and even social gatherings.

We started to sell the cards, and the feedback began to roll in from everywhere. Teachers use them with students who have trouble opening up about themselves, and I have a friend who hosts a monthly dinner and leaves a card on every guest's plate as a way of sparking new and deeper conversations around the table. We even have a few clients who have bought them in bulk and distributed them to their entire organization.

I discovered that not only are the cards great at provoking deeper connections, but they are permission-granting tools as well. If I were at a cocktail party, met someone I didn't know, and asked him or her, "Where do you feel most nurtured?" he or she would probably think I was a creep. But when the cards are involved and they are the ones asking the question, people become more open-minded. I've seen it happen countless times. Complete strangers pair up and start working with the cards, and within minutes someone is crying, laughing hysterically, or gesticulating wildly as they relay an impassioned anecdote about their life. The cards create space for connections to occur and empathy to emerge. People begin to understand each other on a deeper level.

One day I got a text from a good friend who lives in San Francisco. He told me he had been dating a woman for about half a year, and they had decided to take a road trip down Highway 1, riding along the coast from San Francisco to Los Angeles.

He had taken his Q&E deck with him for the drive, and he and his girlfriend had started to go through all the questions together.

The message he sent had a photo from when they had pulled over on a turnout in Big Sur. The big blue Pacific Ocean was in the background, and in the foreground was his girlfriend smiling with tears running down her face. He said the cards had let them get deeper in a few hours than they had gotten in six months of dating.

I realize that this anecdote might seem a little sappy for a business book, but here's the point: these archetypes have plenty of applications in our lives. Sometimes we forget that "business-people" and "colleagues" are real people, too. I've sat in countless meetings where clients have told us about their need to focus on business-to-business conversations—omitting the very obvious point that when their customers leave their office, they are regular people just like you and me. Though you will likely use the principles in this book at work, don't be surprised if they also find their way into helping you connect with empathy in many other situations.

The Empathic Archetypes and the Whole Self together created a sort of powerful alchemy that spurs empathy. It's hard to say why or how that happened, but time and again I have seen people change as they play with these cards and probe into territories we rarely reach during the small talk we all engage in. Give it a try, and see what emerges as you take a deeper look into those around you and, ultimately, into yourself.

CHAPTER THREE EXERCISES

— Five-Minute Contemplations —

You can glean new insights into your Whole Self through a series of five-minute contemplations designed to engage each of the seven aspects. Whether done in one sitting or incrementally over the course of a week, each of these prompts will nudge you into a deeper, more self-aware state of being, ultimately aiding in a greater sense of empathy for your self and where you find yourself in a given moment in time.

We start at the most tangible level of the self, the physical self.

Physical Self

In a comfortable seated position, close your eyes and take three slow deep breaths. Pay attention only to your physical body. Feel how your chest expands and rises with your inhalation and relaxes on your exhalation. Breathe as slowly as you comfortably can.

After breathing, conduct a "body scan," moving your attention slowly to different parts of your body. For example, when you bring your attention to your feet, don't just feel your feet, but feel everything about your feet. Feel the air around them, the ground below them. Feel the temperature of the room from your feet. Feel your toes and arches and Achilles tendons and everything else you can. The muscles, the skin, the ligaments. Feel every aspect of your feet.

Scan upward from your feet into your legs, your hips, torso, hands, arms, shoulders, neck, and head. Pay attention to what is easy to connect with and what is difficult. How in touch are you with the various parts of your body? Do you feel them as you go through your normal day, or is your physical body just a big vehicle to move your brain around from meeting to meeting? Take the time to move throughout your body and notice its quality. Is it holding tension in a particular place? Do you have discomfort anywhere? How does your body change when you sense it in a seated versus a standing position?

When you finish the scan, take a moment to sense the entirety of your physical body. Take three slow breaths again and open your eyes.

Ask yourself how different you feel about your body relative to how you felt when you began the exercise. Do you have a different awareness for your physicality? Your breath? Take a moment to write down your feelings, and pay attention to how they change as you continue to do this exercise.

Emotional Self

Check in with yourself and ask what emotion you most commonly feel at work / at home / at all times—whatever setting is relevant to you.

Do you find yourself anxious? Distracted? Angry?

Perhaps you're contemplative. Or joyful. Or in love.

Whatever it is, that's the emotion you want to zero in on for this exercise.

Set a timer for five minutes. Without overthinking things, simply connect to that emotion and write down whatever comes up for you as you sit within that state. The writing needs no structure—some of it may be stream of consciousness, while other parts may make great sense. That's totally fine. Just express your emotions on the page.

- Describe how this emotion makes the rest of you feel.
- How often do you feel this way?
- Can you control how often and when you feel this way? Does this emotion control you?
- Are there specific people who trigger this emotion in you? Why do they do so?

As before, there is no right or wrong way to conduct this exercise. Simply stay connected to the emotion and give yourself the space to document it without analysis. Just feel and write whatever comes to the surface.

When the timer goes off, take a few deep breaths, and then read what you've written. Some of it will likely be what you expect, but other parts may surprise you. It's possible you could discover that this is a persistent emotion you don't want controlling your life. Or perhaps it may become clear that there is a trigger (a person, a thing, a circumstance, etc.) that causes this emotion to arise within you. Understanding your emotions and what gives rise to them will ultimately help you manage them more acutely.

You can use this exercise to log your ongoing relationship with a variety of emotions that arise within yourself. All of this information will provide you with opportunities to learn more about your inner world and the shifting tides of your emotional state.

Inspired Self

Some of us find inspiration more easily than others. But like empathy, inspiration is something we cultivate by connecting to it and understanding it, allowing inspiration to become a more familiar state.

To begin, recall a moment when you felt truly inspired. Perhaps it was when you heard someone deliver a pep talk that lit a fire within you. Or maybe it was the time you took a watercolor painting class. It doesn't matter what it was. Just go with it.

Start your timer for five minutes, and focus on your memories of that inspired moment and remember where you were.

- What was the environment like?
- Were you alone or with other people?
- How did it feel when your inspiration began to manifest in action?
- Were you conscious of it at the time, or did it simply take over your actions?

That's the richness of good inspiration: you can't control what happens next. If we're lucky, the power of the Inspired Self takes us on a creative roller-coaster ride, supporting the making, doing, or experiencing of something that truly satisfies our Whole Self.

Ask yourself what about this particular moment brought such inspiration to you. Was it the setting of the moment, or was it a person or even a side of yourself you didn't know existed? What lit the fire within you?

Once you've grasped the elements of this experience, try to determine the aspects of it that you can re-create in order to re-ignite inspiration. Create a short list of no more than three to five things, and use it as your Inspired Self's "cheat sheet" for when you need to drop back into that state.

Maybe a music playlist or a walk in the park inspires you. It could be a phone call with an old friend, a ten-day vipassana meditation at an ashram, or just a great piece of chocolate cake.

Whatever the things are, understand that they are a part of your tool kit and you can utilize them to reconnect with this aspect of your Whole Self.

Community Self

The Community Self is the self that relates to the people around you and they to you. Because of this two-way street, we will divide your time into two parts for this exercise.

For the first two and a half minutes, contemplate what community or communities you spend the most time serving. Your family? Your friends? Your coworkers?

Ask yourself how you feel about providing service to those groups. Do they recharge you or deplete you? Why do you support them in the first place? Do you feel that you have a choice to support them or not?

Write down your answers if you'd like, or simply think these questions through. Some people find that the act of writing their answers helps them concretize their feelings, but if you prefer simply to contemplate these questions, that's fine, too.

Next, flip the question and ask yourself what community or communities support you. Are they the same ones you support? Why or why not? What makes the group(s) so helpful and restorative for you? Do they give you something you don't have within yourself, or do they shine a light on things you already have in abundance?

Taking the time to consider the people around you and the dynamics that cause them to be prominent in your life will undoubtedly present you with powerful insights to help you understand how a key part of your Whole Self interacts with the world around you.

Intellectual Self

Too many of us have a tendency to overuse the Intellectual Self, which controls how we present ourselves through words and concepts. This overuse can manifest itself in talking because we like the sound of our voice or going on and on about big concepts and our perspective on them. Left unchecked, this is the self of an overzealous ego. When balanced against the other selves, however, it helps us calibrate our views with composure and humility.

Take a moment to use the tools you've learned in earlier chapters and look at yourself with as much objectivity as you can. Allow your Intellectual Self to analyze where you are in your life and the pursuit of your ambitions.

- Do you feel you are where you wanted to be five years ago?
- Are you satisfied with your personal growth? With your life's trajectory?

- What traits emerge when you sense your ego or personality begin to enlarge itself?
- Why does that happen?

Give your Intellectual Self permission to ask objective questions that challenge your worldview, and in equal measure do the same with your personal state. Contemplate tough questions, not just easy ones. Challenge yourself to consider things you don't want to confront. Doing so will lead you to the most honest and literal appraisal of where you stand and what path you've taken in your life.

Allow this exercise to reset your expectations or ambitions. The Intellectual Self can reorient you when it's necessary, and you will continue to adjust your heading as you walk along life's path. Don't feel obliged to hold on to things that no longer serve you. Instead, embrace this exercise as a permission-granting moment to take a fresh look at yourself and chart a course for your future.

Mindful Self

The Mindful Self is attuned to presence. The previous exercises have focused on individually sensing your physical body, emotions, feelings, and thoughts. Now you will let go of this compartmentalizing and acknowledge all of those states at the same time.

Those of you who are already meditators may find this exercise similar to your existing practice.

Get yourself into a comfortable seated position and begin with three slow, deep breaths.

Gently close your eyes and allow your thoughts to drop away. Sense the present moment without internal dialogue or thought.

When thoughts arise, and they will, acknowledge them. You see, the mind is built to think. That's what it does most often, so thoughts are inevitable.

In this meditation, we are developing a different relationship to our thoughts. We aren't dwelling on them or allowing them to go on forever. Instead, we use this time to notice when a thought occurs, and we take a moment to acknowledge it.

You might even find it helpful to label your thoughts. You might label some as "thinking" or "inner dialogue." The point is to notice them, feeling any emotions or sensations associated with them, and then return to the present.

This acknowledgment and return to the present are work you do with your Mindful Self as you continue strengthening your comfort with self-observation and presence.

Once you've completed this meditation, take a moment to make notes about any experiences you had. You may find it helpful to observe how easy or difficult it was to maintain a state of self-observation. Notice if this exercise is easier for you to do in the morning versus the evening, at home versus at work. Assessing these variables will help give you greater insight into your own state of mindfulness and what is helping or hindering your ability to maintain it regularly.

Aspirational Self

The Aspirational Self is really the culmination of the good work you put into the earlier exercises and an acknowledgement that your other selves are in alignment.

The Japanese call this self your *ikigai*, or reason for being.

Ask yourself if you have a sense of what this might be. For many of us, this idea is elusive and hard to pin down.

If you are already clear about your life's greatest purpose, congratulations; you're better off than most of us. But many of us are still searching or evolving our view as our lives change with time. Consider each aspect of your Whole Self as you explore your Aspirational Self. Use the diagram below to help map this aspect of your Whole Self.

Map the aspects of your own life, and see where the intersections occur. At the heart of these four parts, you'll find the core of your Aspirational Self.

Once you discover what this is, you'll have found your North Star, of sorts. Use it to orient your future decisions, ensuring that the choices you make are consistent with this ultimate aspect of your Whole Self and that you serve your personal pursuit of satisfaction and greater purpose.

Empathy Journal: Bringing the Whole Self and the Empathic Archetypes Together

I wanted to integrate the Seven Selves with the Seven Archetypes, and that naturally led to seven questions for each archetype, with each question inspired by one of the seven selves. This exercise is incredibly valuable, though it is a long one.

Those of you who are willing to undertake it will find that it dramatically helps evolve your perspective on empathy.

This exercise takes fifty days and begins with taking a moment to write down your definition of empathy and what it means to you.

Next identify which archetype you feel you are most closely aligned with and then the next, on through the other five, ending up with the archetype in whose behaviors you feel you are most deficient.

On the second day, go to the first question for your first archetype from the lists that begin on page 82. Answer this question, and capture your answer in the journal. On the second day, you will do the same for the second question, proceeding until all forty-nine have been addressed.

On day fifty, take a moment to capture your evolved definition of empathy and its meaning in your life.

CHAPTER FOUR

Showing Up

"I love that brand's products."

"That organization is far and away the best in the industry."

"That company is praised for how it treats its employees."

There they are: brand, organization, and company. They spill from our lips regularly when we talk about businesses and their products. But we're missing something—or overlooking it—when we talk in this way. Whether consciously or subconsciously, we are forgetting that a "company" isn't doing any of those things—it's the people inside the company who make everything happen.

We know that companies are made up of people, which might seem like an overly simplistic observation. But the language most people use to talk about the business world often leaves out the people at the heart of companies. The more empathic versions are these:

"I've loved every product its designers create."

"That team is far and away the best in the industry."

"The leaders of that company are praised for how they treat their employees."

Notice a difference? When we speak about the people within the business, not just the business itself, we add a layer of recognition and understanding of exactly whom or what we are talking about. And that's a critical element to bear in mind as we start to think about building more effective, more empathic companies. It starts with the people inside.

When we recognize that people are at the core of every business, it becomes necessary that we show up in a different way. If we simply "phone it in," our behavior has an impact on the company. But when we bring our best selves to the companies we serve, we can often create some pretty spectacular results.

This isn't just something that comes from the top down. Yes, a CEO certainly has a major role to play in establishing an organization's culture and environment, but he or she is not the only one responsible. Working with companies as small as ours and others with nearly a million employees worldwide, I've noted one important element that always plays a role in building a strong internal culture: *alignment*.

When a company's purpose is understood—truly understood at a strategic and emotional level—it permeates everything the organization does.

SEEKING ALIGNMENT

The leaders of a global retail bank asked us to help them raise awareness of the CEO's new mission among all their employees. They had hundreds of thousands of people worldwide who were going into work less engaged than they might have been because they didn't have a sense of *why* they were going to work. Sure, they may have been clear about what job function they performed, but they didn't know what that work meant to the company's greater purpose, the larger goal they were all working toward. Employees of companies with great alignment are able to answer those questions quickly and easily.

One of my favorite examples of this happened eighteen years before I was born, in 1962, at NASA's Launch Operations Center on Merritt Island, Florida. The story goes that President John F. Kennedy, who the year before had established an ambitious goal of putting a man on the moon by the end of the decade, was touring the center. At one point he saw a janitor carrying a broom past the tour group. Kennedy stopped the man and said, "Hi, I'm Jack Kennedy. What do you do here?" The man responded, "Well, I'm helping put a man on the moon."

That is alignment. Whether this anecdote is true or apocryphal, the point is still clear: this is what it feels like when a company's mission permeates into every corner of a business. People aren't simply coming to work to perform a specific function; they are showing up, in the broadest sense of the term, bringing their full self to the entirety of the business and its mission.

The best companies do this so well that it becomes infectious. A great culture supports and encourages its team members to "show up" every day because having their full, talented selves present will make everyone better. I've had the good fortune of seeing this in action with some of the companies we work with, and it has also been true with my own business as we've evolved our own purpose and practice. It's powerful stuff.

EVERYBODY SHOWING UP

We began our relationship with Nike well before our work on Hyperfeel. It was a damp springtime afternoon when I drove onto the Nike campus for the first time. As I turned into the main gate, I was greeted warmly by the security guard at his station. He seemed like a character you'd encounter on the grounds of Disney World, not the gatekeeper at a corporate office. He smiled and asked if I'd been to the campus before. I told him it was my first time, and he gave me a knowing look, the way someone does when he knows you're in for a treat. I pulled into a massive parking lot and noticed a series of signs at the front. One of them read, "Reserved for Michael Jordan." I was starstruck before I'd even made it out of the parking lot.

I parked my car humbly, a few rows away from Michael Jordan's spot, and went to meet my clients.

Right away I noticed memorabilia from many of Nike's athletes on display, but I also saw that Nike employees were being celebrated in the same way. I wasn't just looking at a framed jersey from an Olympic gold medal soccer team; I was seeing the cleats designed on this campus for the athlete who had worn the jersey. The athlete and the people who had created the product were on the same pedestal. There were photos from the innovation sessions alongside photos of the athlete on the playing field. The way it was presented, sharing both sides of the story, made it clear that the medal had been won because everyone had shown up.

Over the years that we've worked with the Nike brand, I've always been impressed by the company's knack for demonstrating that everyone's role is important. Everyone is part of the team. And everyone is expected to show up and give his or her best. The company culture has a definite athleticism, and it extends way beyond physically playing sports. Employees do play sports and work out together, and the campus is beautifully designed with soccer fields, putting greens, gyms, tracks and more, but the sense of teamwork comes through in the way they speak to one another and engage in work. It's spirited, and I've been in conference room meetings with them that felt like a locker room before a big game. The teams I've worked with at Nike were aligned to the greater mission established by the company's founders.

Nike's mission is "To bring inspiration and innovation to every athlete in the world." When Nike cofounder Bill Bowerman was asked to define "athlete," he said, "If you have a body, you're an athlete." That is why Nike's culture is so powerful. Bowerman democratized athleticism. You might not be the next LeBron James or Serena Williams, but you're still important to the brand. Your ability to perform better and more comfortably, to have empathy for your inner athlete no matter your skill level, is meaningful. And the fact that the company's employees understand that importance, and come to work every day, whether it's in marketing, design, or accounting, is what makes its culture so powerful.

But doing what Nike does is not easy. There are challenges to building an empathic culture in an environment as demanding and high intensity as Nike's. After all, it is an athletic wear company. The teams work hard, and they expect the best from their colleagues. It's not for everyone. In our time working for clients that have strong alignment, I've seen people leave because they weren't the right fit. And that's okay. Not every organization is a perfect fit for every employee. This sort of tension often arises when a company's culture starts to become more clearly defined, felt, and lived by its people.

ONE COMPANY, MANY SIDES

Empathic company cultures help teams understand their external audiences—groups such as shareholders, the media, consumers, and more—but they can influence the internal audience as well.

Such companies, and the teams within them, know how to connect their mission with all of their different audiences in a meaningful way.

Imagine that your company is a cube, with its six sides each representing a part that contributes to the whole. The sides might be things such as your product, the company's financial health, its internal culture, and so on. Together they make your company whole.

Empathic employees in an organization know that all sides are important, but they also know which side connects best and most crucially with each particular audience. If a reporter from the *Financial Times* sits down with a CEO, it makes sense that he or she is looking for sound bites about the company's financials. But if the same CEO was being interviewed by a reporter from *Fast Company* or *Harvard Business Review*, it wouldn't be appropriate to focus only on financials, as those sorts of publications often report on a variety of topics related to business. Thus the reporter might be looking for a more nuanced picture of the CEO or a better sense of the company's culture. That's an empathic behavior I've often seen lacking in the leaders of companies. Too often, people have been overly trained to cover the points *they* want to talk about with the media and what *they* think is most important, with little consideration for what the interviewer might want to discuss. Empathically meeting a reporter's needs early in the conversation increases the chances that he or she will feel understood. It also builds trust, as the reporter will likely sense that you understand the publication and its objective. That, in turn, can often create empathy in the other direction—piquing the curiosity of the reporter and giving the interviewee room to discuss other aspects of the business that he or she deems important. This isn't complicated, but it *is* a muscle many leaders don't train often enough.

I host a monthly podcast at Sub Rosa called *Applied Empathy*, which we record in front of a live audience. Every month, we bring in two to four people who have a specific point of view, and we dig into it with them, looking to reveal different perspectives, different "sides of the cube" of topics such as beauty, creativity, or wellness. Moderating is something I've come to enjoy, but I found it difficult in the beginning because I was coming up against the same tension I described in the example of the reporter. Some panelists can't help but try to steer the conversation toward a talking point they want to get across.

As a moderator, my job is to keep us on topic while also empathically trying to bring out new and different views of a story that our listeners want to hear. Our most successful podcasts have been the ones that give listeners the fullest picture of a topic. The more diverse the panelists, the more conflicting their views, the better the audience responds. Our listeners gain a more all-encompassing sense of empathy for a topic or an industry when they can hear about it from all of its different sides.

The same is true within companies. The best leaders act empathically toward all sides of their business, and they do the same toward the company's key audiences. Your company might be as simple as a cube or as complex as a dodecahedron. It doesn't matter; the work is still the same. It takes time to understand each audience—to get outside of your own perspective and see the company from the point of view of investors, media, employees, potential employees, and more. Once you do, you can more deftly uncover gaps in the company's messaging, misalignments in its operations, or dysfunctions in its culture. All sides of the business need to work in harmony, aligned toward the same mission and goals.

EXCAVATING EMPATHY

Sometimes at Sub Rosa we do this work overtly. We talk to different audiences about the product or service being offered. It's important to focus on their perspective as a way of figuring out why they feel the way they do. This kind of investigative work, which involves letting go of preconceptions, can be difficult for people inside the company because their closeness to the intricacies of the business can create blind spots. But with practice it is doable, and a good tool for this is the Empathic Archetypes, which help people assume different perspectives and behaviors as a way of shaking them out of any overly defined point of view they may have.

The Cultivator, for example, whose behavior is to "commit" and see the long game, can be a helpful perspective to assume when important near-term decisions need to be made. At moments like this, we often focus on what the immediate ramifications will be. How will this decision change my business today? Tomorrow? In the next quarter? People rarely zoom out several years ahead to consider how a decision today will be felt then. But doing so can provide helpful insights. Big thinkers such as Steve Jobs and Elon Musk have often acted as Cultivators. Their bets have always been big, far-reaching, and based on where they see the world going in five, ten, maybe even twenty-plus years' time. It's a perspective that doesn't come naturally to everyone, but with training and repetition, it can help you see your desired future state more clearly.

Leaders must also act as Seekers, daring and unafraid to take risks or pivot. Not bringing this sort of behavior into a business will leave it struggling to keep up in the rapidly changing world around it.

There are times, however, when empathic insights can be gathered more covertly. Direct conversation isn't always a feasible way to get the information needed to gain new perspective and plan your business or team's next move. Sometimes people are reluctant to share their experiences or thoughts. When this occurs, you may have to try "undercover" techniques (such as being a secret shopper at a rival's store) in order to get the information you need. Edward de Bono is a well-known proponent of parallel thinking, in which a participant supports his or her point of view on the subject while others present their own perspective. De Bono is the creator of the "Six Thinking Hats" method for carrying out this parallel thinking through role play.

Unlike the more common dialectic approach, in which two people debate a point from opposing positions (e.g., the prosecutor and defense attorney in a courtroom), in parallel thinking participants inhabit assigned roles and they analyze the topic from various sides. De Bono's "Six Thinking Hats" method uses six colored "hats" we can wear when we need to think about problems. The blue hat, for example, focuses on managerial questions, such as "What is the goal of this?" The black hat is more focused on logic, using caution and realism to determine flaws and evaluate ideas. Each "hat" presents us with a way of looking at a particular situation in isolation from our own perspective. The challenge in this work comes in playing a role that may be contrary to your own instincts, but it can be essential to making sure you're not just "getting high on your own supply" and falling in love with ideas based on your cognitive biases.

The same is true for the Empathic Archetypes. Though we all have the capacity to think from all seven different archetypes' perspectives, changing from one to another comfortably takes practice. But the exercise will give you a more holistic understanding of a topic, a problem, or your business, which lets you see it in its entirety and, just as important, shows you what it is not.

Any attempts to create alignment within your business are essentially a clarification of what you are and what you are not. During this process, a period of integration can occur, during which some people step up and fly the new mission's banner while others reject it, disagree with it, disengage from the work or their team, or simply resign. You have to expect and accept uncomfortable moments during a time of change or transformation, yet still know the work is essential to any company's success. To function empathically and effectively, the leaders of a company must have a clear understanding of its mission and goals, its audiences, and their needs—and the company culture must be in alignment.

FROM COWORKING TO LIFELONG LEARNING

Many of the companies we work with are large, complex multinationals, but we also get to work with the leaders of new, progressive companies seeking to disrupt an industry and create new models for success. One of those is General Assembly.

General Assembly (GA) started as a coworking space in New York City. It was a beautifully designed, 10,000-square-foot full floor located in Manhattan's Flatiron district, a bustling neighborhood sometimes dubbed "Silicon Alley" because of its concentration of high-tech companies, similar to the San Francisco Bay Area's Silicon Valley. The neighborhood has been a home to hot-to-trot start-ups for years, and GA was located right in the center of it.

The company built up a good business leasing desk space to

many start-ups that weren't ready for their own office or whose owners found the camaraderie of a shared space more to their liking. GA provided the snack stations, coffee machines, and common areas appointed with eccentrically shaped and colored seating that have become the norm in most start-up offices, making the space a thriving community.

But the 10,000 square feet filled up fast, and GA didn't have room for more tenants. At the same time, it opened a few similar spaces in other cities and the same thing happened. The company could have taken more space on other floors or in other buildings, but its founders knew they would no longer be a community but a real estate business, which wasn't their goal. They needed to take on the Seeker archetype and think about a pivot.

That caused them to stumble upon a perk they'd been offering their tenants: weekly programs that included lecturers, teachers, workshop organizers, and skills trainers. Some classes were even taught by the start-up tenants. There was great demand for the programs, which people loved, so the founders began a hard pivot toward a new business model centered around skills development and training.

GA slowly let its leases with existing tenants expire, and as square footage became available, it expanded its educational programming to include technology development, data, design, and business training. Demand continued to be high, and soon the classes were oversubscribed. The feedback from students was great, but still the brand needed help articulating its new mission.

That was when we were brought aboard.

In applying empathy, our work started with conversations among the leadership team, the staff, instructors, and students as well as several of the company's investors. As we'd seen before, things can become challenging for a company's culture in such moments of change. While GA's leaders were redefining what the company was, they couldn't help but define what it was not. Some of the GA staff had signed on to work at a coworking space, and now that the company was in the education business, they saw that their skills didn't match with what the new business required.

Our conversations with GA students told us that even though they got a lot out of the programs, they felt a lack of community. Interestingly, the center of the company's coworking business had somehow been stripped out of the education business. Students told us that when they were in a class, they had a sense of community, but once it finished, there was no way to stay tethered to GA or the people they'd met. GA (and its competitors) needed to realize something that colleges and universities have known for years: that your alumni are your strongest allies.

Our goal was to help the company develop a new mission that would broaden its focus from ad hoc course work and education to a mission we called "lifelong learning." Anyone who works in the start-up and technology world knows how important it is to update one's skills regularly—at least as often as new programming languages crop up (which is pretty often these days). The same is true with design software and user experience and even business modeling. We guided GA to stand up and commit to all of its students, past, present, and future, promising to be their lifelong learning partner. GA would dedicate itself to maintaining relationships with its alums and ensure that it would be there for them anytime they needed to level up their career, take a step toward a new skill, or even connect with other people who have the skills needed for a particular business.

This was a new way of thinking about the company. GA's brand and marketing team now had to expand beyond the new-student acquisition market to maintaining contact with alumni, building a network of students from campuses around the world, and designing a physical space so that no matter what GA space a person was in, from New York to Melbourne, he or she would have the feeling of being part of the same family.

Our team worked side by side with GA to develop a new brand system, evolving the logo and other elements from its coworking days in ways that aligned to the new mission we'd created. The internal culture galvanized as the language became more and more real. People began to speak differently about what GA did in a way that was aligned to a mission that felt real and connected to the community it served.

This alignment showed up in the words the leadership team used when communicating with their alumni and current students, and, most important, it was part of the services GA was delivering. The GA team understood what parts of the company's story would appeal to the media and its investor community, and the company quickly became a press darling as a leader in the field of continuing education. They also discovered that this work helped them recruit new talent into the organization with skills that were aligned to the brand as well as a dedication to service, education, and community.

In six short months, as the alignment was realized, the GA brand evolved into something new while still retaining important parts from its past. The company's spaces around the world felt united visually and evoked the sense of community we all envisioned. And most important, GA's students and alumni were being engaged in a deeper, more meaningful way. They knew that GA was committed to being a partner to them as they grew in their career. It was a beautiful thing to watch, and it showed us that when we work with empathy—getting a comprehensive picture of the business from all sides—great things are bound to happen.

FOUR TENSIONS

The work we did to help General Assembly change its business had powerful results, but not every company is ready to accept change, and even the ones that say they are often discover that it's not as easy as they'd hoped. That's because one of the hardest things to change is entrenched behavior, especially if your organization is not set up for it.

In my years working with companies and organizations, I have observed four key tensions that consistently emerge as stumbling blocks and can slow down the change process. The only way to get past them is to approach them with empathy for where the business is today and where it wants to go. This will ultimately give you powerful insights into how your organization is presently organized and what shifts might be necessary in order to bring about the right changes. These four tensions are:

- Objective versus subjective decision-making
- Top-down versus bottom-up culture
- Human-centered versus ecosystemic thinking
- Passive versus proactive leadership

These are not binary choices. No company can be wholly one or the other. Instead, think of them as a spectrum. As you read the next section, consider the distinctions between each and where your company currently sits on the spectrum. It's useful to understand this so you can identify where improvements can be made to help make your culture and your company accept empathy more readily.

It's important to remember that no organization can effectively practice empathy in a vacuum. Empathy reveals big, complex, and nuanced topics that draw in the larger world. As leaders throughout a company make decisions, they need to keep in mind "close to home" things such as the company's culture and team dynamics while also considering the outside social, political, and economic climates, which can be hard to measure, making it sometimes difficult to determine how much they directly relate to the business. But balancing them strategically allows empathy to be built into the organization, often with profound results.

OBJECTIVE VERSUS SUBJECTIVE
DECISION-MAKING

Objective decision-making is relatively simple to get a handle on. When a problem is approached objectively, facts are considered without feelings or bias to confuse them. Either things happen, or they don't. A light switch works, or it doesn't. A train is on schedule, or it isn't. If the solution is clear and factual, objectivity is easy to come by.

The problem is that today's businesses, and our roles within them, need to operate more and more on subjectivity. And subjective decision-making takes some getting used to. When things are subjective, there can be multiple right answers, which can be influenced by a person's feelings and biases, which can lead to confusion and indecision. Perspective, personal taste, intuition, and a host of other individualized attributes play a role in making subjective decisions.

Take, for example, the hiring of a new team member. You've objectively narrowed the candidates through your requirements for a university degree, industry experience, and specific hard skills.

Two finalists come in for interviews, and now everything will depend on subjective decision-making. This is likely something you already do instinctively: you evaluate prospective employees' cultural fit and presentation style, even how they make you feel when you talk with them (whether you consciously recognize that or not). Even knowing what you want to see in the candidates, it can still be hard to make a subjective decision. For example, let's say the first of the two candidates walks in with confidence, looks you straight in the eyes, and answers questions directly but doesn't offer anything exactly memorable, while the second candidate is a little meek, fumbles with their résumé holder, and makes little eye contact but does answer your questions with depth and passion.

It's not an easy choice. You must know the type of person who will thrive in the company culture as well as what skills are needed versus those that are nice to have. An insecure candidate might not thrive in an aggressive culture. Ultimately, a hiring decision comes down to having an empathic read on the candidates relative to the organization. It's a subjective call to make but one that will have real consequences.

One way to approach subjective decision-making is to consider what factors are important to the decision and put them into a hierarchy. Taking the example above, we might say that cultural fit within the company is highly important, along with other considerations such as writing style, creativity, and demeanor. The interviewer will evaluate each of those factors through his or her own perspective. Perhaps they shouldn't all be weighted equally. For example, it is best to know from the outset if the interviewer's opinion of the candidate's creativity is more important than that of his or her ability to fit into the company culture.

The same could be said when evaluating ideas presented by your team for a new marketing campaign. What's most important to you? How an ad looks? How it reads? What you think your consumers will think of it? What your boss will think of it? Giving all of those considerations equal weight can be overwhelming and prevent you from making a decision. Well-informed decisions are best made after you determine what subjective criteria matter the most (and what don't) so that your empathic intuition can be directed at the right things.

Decision-Making in Action

In 2015, I was invited to visit Princeton University as a guest speaker to talk about empathy and how it can be used to solve problems. The students' feedback was so positive that the university approached Sub Rosa about creating a class on the topic. We had never created a curriculum centered around empathy, but we jumped at the chance to immerse ourselves deeper in the topic than we'd ever been.

We called the class Empathic Design because we wanted students to understand that "design" is much broader than what people typically think when they hear the word. We design everything—products, cultures, services, and so on. We knew we wanted to give the students a perspective that would open the aperture on design. The more design thinkers we have out in the world making things work better and behaving more empathically, the better off we'll all be.

We based our curriculum on our experiences developing brand and business solutions for clients so the students would be able to see empathy being applied practically in the real world. The class was offered through Princeton's Keller Center for Innovation in Engineering Education, and the majority of the students were studying mechanical engineering, computer science, and entrepreneurship. The students came with a wide range of disciplines and approaches to problem-solving, which led to an interesting tension in the class of comfort and discomfort with objective versus subjective decision-making.

Through a mix of readings, case-based learning, and participatory labs, our budding young empaths would work through a series of challenges, not unlike the exercises in this book, that taught them how to apply empathy in order to become more and more comfortable with subjective work—which for many of them was foreign territory.

Mechanical engineering, for instance, though at times dependent on subjective choices, is most often evaluated objectively. Either a machine works, or it doesn't. Either it performs its desired task, or it fails. The *way* it performs its task could be described in subjective terms, but most of our students majoring in mechanical engineering were comfortable with mechanically engineered solutions that could be judged objectively by the results they achieved.

Straightforward computational and analysis-based code, from our computer science majors, is also evaluated objectively by whether or not the task was performed, but app development, on which so many of today's computer science students are focused, depends on a programmer's ability to make a variety of both objective and subjective choices. The best apps are solidly engineered (meaning that they don't crash and they run efficiently), but they also offer alluring interfaces and an appealing user experience. This sort of app design is in high demand and represents the confluence of great objective and subjective skills manifesting in a single product.

Students in the entrepreneurial program especially needed to hone their proficiency in subjective decision-making. No doubt about it, entrepreneurs must know when to remain objective, but great entrepreneurs rely on their subjective skills to push their ideas, teams, and businesses to greater heights. Our entrepreneurial students knew how valuable this skill was for them, and many of them took our class to try to improve this part of their thinking.

Even though our class was taught at the Keller school, it was open to enrollment campuswide, so it was also peppered with budding philosophers, architects, political scientists, and economists. No matter where the students came from at the university, we saw that the ones who could step outside of their own shoes and see problems from varied perspectives were the ones who could most readily recognize opportunities for improvement. They were also able to grapple gracefully with the paradox of choice among multiple right answers better than their peers who could not.

Early on, we got the students involved in a real-world experiment that called on subjective decision-making. We sent them to a part of Princeton's main street and asked them to report back on the specific design flaws they saw there. We also wanted them to suggest improvements that could be made. Typically they went out in small groups and observed traffic patterns, how pedestrians moved around the neighborhood, the types of stores that lined the street, and other key elements. With few exceptions, each student returned to class convinced that he or she had discovered the most important and flawed aspects of the town's design. To their surprise, they found that many of their peers had identified the same issues and had reached similar if not exactly the same solutions.

This was often our first step in teaching Applied Empathy: helping students see that they were looking at problems from only their own perspective. Their inability to step outside themselves prevented them from going further than scratching the surface of the underlying design challenges and caused them to miss the chance to be more creative with their solutions. After all, there are only so many ways you can address a lack of late-night dining options or a shortage of available bike racks (two common complaints of any college-age student).

We then sent them back to look more deeply and see what they could discover when they peered beyond the obvious. We asked them to take on different personas, to consider life in Princeton from a perspective greater than their own. Some went out and looked at the town from the perspective of a mom with kids and found opportunities for better stroller parking outside stores. Others looked at the town through the eyes of the elderly, noticing that much of the town center was designed for the young academic community but lacked certain accommodations for older residents. Some students even interviewed the subjects they were observing. The deeper they went, the stronger their insights became, and this sort of immersive research quickly demonstrated the array of solutions they could reach by utilizing empathy.

Our goal in the class (and in this book) was to teach the tools needed to process information differently and more diversely. The students learned to gather insights and important information from potential users, audiences, and customers, and also how to develop more complete, well-rounded solutions—as I hope you will. The class ended with the presentation of a semester-long group project that challenged teams to take on a real-life campus issue and suggest an empathically designed solution. We saw students make hard choices about what problem to tackle, what data and insights to trust, and ultimately what solution to put forward.

Becoming comfortable with subjectivity is one of the most important first steps in harnessing the power of empathy. It's as true as it was for the students at Princeton as it is for the managers and leaders of every company we work with. Empathy for the people around you—be they customers, clients, employees, teammates, or family members—provides critical levels of understanding that will help you make subjective choices from a more informed place, ultimately making them more effective.

TOP-DOWN VERSUS BOTTOM-UP CULTURE

Leaders wanting to build a more empathic company must grapple with how information and decisions flow within their organization and how that process may need to change so that empathy can play a bigger role. The two classic examples of misalignment in this area are top-down and bottom-up cultures. The first comes from a rigid command-and-control structure, with directives flowing from above and being implemented unquestioningly throughout the organization. Top-down organizations often benefit from the efficiencies of having only a few decision makers. But they can also struggle with low employee engagement and morale if individuals feel they have no real influence or sense of agency.

We have also worked with bottom-up companies that seek feedback from teams in both formal and informal ways. These organizations sometimes cultivate stronger, more inclusive cultures, but they can also struggle with too much information coming into the system, putting senior leaders into a state of "analysis paralysis"—unsure of what to do and where to go based on mixed or divergent feedback. This sort of culture often exists in start-ups that have grown quickly and expanded their teams by sometimes as much as ten or a hundred times in only a few years. They began as most start-ups do—leanly. In the beginning they had a small, nimble group of people, and decisions were often made by consensus. The team talked out every major decision because all of its members were invested in getting the company off the ground. As a company grows and head count swells, the old culture of decision by committee may still be seen as democratic and "millennial-minded," but too much of it can destroy a team's ability to make any real decisions.

A top-down business, which often focuses on efficiency and clarity, has the advantage of providing its teams with clear, direct marching orders they can understand and adopt easily. However, we often hear employees in these companies say they don't feel their "voice is being heard," and intuitively, one would think that a rigid, top-down organization squashes the spirit of those who work there and creates a "cog" mentality. But many companies operate successfully with this structure—and some employees even tell us they sought out a culture like this because they could do their job more efficiently and would have clarity about their place in the company and how it operates.

The bottom-up company picks up empathy points for elevating the voices of the whole organization and for taking employees' perspectives into account when decisions are made. But it can be challenging to run a business, particularly a large one, from the bottom up.

Some companies have used technology to add a layer of input into the company. A tech start-up that we worked with, which had more than a thousand employees, installed a series of buttons at the office exit. Each button was a response to the question "How was your day?" Each day the "pulse" of the company was delivered to senior leaders so they had a sense of employees' morale and how recent decisions were affecting the company's culture.

Do I think this tactic on its own is a particularly effective way to run a company from the bottom up? Not really. Will this feature have a major impact on decision-making throughout the organization? Perhaps. But it is an example of the effort some companies are making to stay connected and to create some sort of feedback loop that puts bottom-up information on leadership's radar.

In reality, few organizations are strictly one or the other, and most operate with elements of both.

Constant Calibration

It's important that a company's leaders consider where they are in the life cycle of their business and where their company is in its growth and trajectory. As empathy is applied during growth periods, it can create information overload for decision makers, making it even more important that they have a clear perspective on how much top down versus bottom up they want for their business.

An effective corporate culture, if designed and communicated effectively, should behave like a magnet, attracting behaviors and talent that are aligned to the culture and repelling those that are not. And repelling is a good thing. It means you're being clear about who you are and what you expect from people. Leaders looking for a one-size-fits-all company culture will find themselves disappointed time and again. Culture is an evolutionary element of a business, and over time it will change to accommodate the organization and its needs.

I saw this at Sub Rosa during one of our most pivotal growth spurts. We were doubling our head count from twenty-five to fifty employees pretty rapidly and moving our studio to a new, larger space to accommodate the expansion. It was an exciting time, and it was encouraging to see the company grow at such a pace. But we were also losing some of our top talent.

Many of the people who had been with us the longest wanted to move up into positions that earned more money, most of them managerial. That presented us with a challenge because some were more talented as "makers" than as managers. We were looking for creative solutions to help them find their right place in the company. In some instances we proposed giving them an increase in compensation without changing their responsibilities. We were effectively giving them an opportunity to make more money by continuing to do what they did best.

It felt like a good idea that could give us room to evolve our culture—to empower legacy team members while also bringing in new leaders. To me, it also seemed like a pretty empathic approach, and I was convinced we were onto something.

It didn't work.

Some members of our team were confident that they could manage as well as they made, and they insisted on pursuing new positions. The pressure, the various responsibilities, the company's change from a smaller, scrappy entity to whatever we were becoming brought on some major challenges both culturally and operationally, and eventually we lost some of our early power players.

That was devastating to me and went against the familial spirit I had tried to develop for the company.

One day, I went out for a drink with Jeff Kempler, Sub Rosa's chief operations officer, to talk through some things that were weighing on me. Jeff has seen the inner workings of a lot of different companies over the years. Before coming to Sub Rosa, he had held senior executive positions at music and entertainment multinationals and gaming companies, and he had been a practicing attorney for more than a decade. He had been particularly focused on working with creative individuals in the film and music industries, so his empathy for the type of talent in our business was pretty spot-on. He was around forty-eight years old at the time, going into his second year at Sub Rosa. He was a trusted confidant with a brain too big for his head and a heart to match. I was a young founder, and I was happy to have a thought partner like Jeff in moments like this.

I asked him why we were losing people whom we were wholly invested in trying to retain. I had hoped to see them grow and thrive with us. I couldn't figure it out. What had we done wrong? Why were they resigning?

Jeff drew up a perfectly fitting analogy of the evolution of our company's culture. He said that in a company's early days, the founder is the sun. The founder provides light and warmth to help the company grow. He (in my case) is also a big force that holds the planets in orbit. Without the founder, all the planets would spin out, and the solar system would cease to exist.

But as a company grows, it is often impossible for one person to remain the sun. It is frequently too much responsibility. And that was happening for us.

Jeff recognized how disappointing it was to lose those team members, but he insisted that it was an inevitable part of growth and that, in the end, more and more leaders would emerge and contribute to playing the role of the "sun" in our solar system. In truth, that was already happening. Jeff was one of them, along with our CFO, Julie Puccio, who had earned my trust years earlier and had moved up the ranks from a midlevel position to one of my most trusted thought partners.

As we talked more about that analogy, it became our shared goal for the business. It seemed like the right thing to do, and it gave me permission to delegate some responsibility and let me focus on growing the business instead of running the company's day-to-day operations. But in time it would also be unhealthy for our management team to be alone at the center. We wanted all the leaders in the company to feel that they had influence and to know that collectively, each of us had a meaningful place in the "solar system."

Jeff was right. The company was changing, and as a result, we needed a new culture.

After a rocky year passed, we hit our stride, and things felt great again. There was a new sense of leadership emanating from new people we brought in with fresh thinking, as well as support from some of our leaders who were with us for the long haul. I was no longer the sun holding everything in orbit. Neither was Jeff or Julie. We were surrounded by passionate people who believed in the mission we had articulated, and we all wanted to share the responsibility for making that vision a reality.

This sort of thing doesn't happen just once in growing companies; it happens often, and good leaders anticipate such changes and are undaunted by them. Change is inevitable. By being aware of it and embracing it with openness and empathy, we can calibrate our strategy quickly and effectively in order to meet the needs of the business.

Empathic companies train dexterity into the fabric of their culture. They have a true understanding of the dynamics at play on a variety of levels within the organization, and they know that great cultures are built by constantly calibrating the top-down aspects of their operations with the bottom-up feedback from the organization as a whole. Applying empathy to an organization or team is a constantly evolving process, but with careful attention, it can inspire and empower leaders to steward the company through change time and again. And again and again.

HUMAN-CENTERED VERSUS
ECOSYSTEMIC THINKING

"Human-centered design" is a philosophy that creates solutions expressly designed for a specific audience. "Ecosystemic thinking" refers to a group of interrelated elements working together. They are ten-dollar marketing terms that have been bandied around so often that they have lost a lot of their power. But in working our way through the tension between them, we can learn a great deal about more fully harnessing the powers of empathy.

Human-centered design is a cornerstone of modern design theory. Popularized and refined by IDEO more than thirty years ago, this form of thinking incorporates a variety of human factors and usability studies into the design of any product or service. Look no further than the safety caps on your prescription medicines or the mouse you use to navigate your computer to see how important human-centered design thinking has been to problem-solving.

But the increased popularity of human-centered design has often caused it to be seen as the solution to all problems instead of being just one ingredient in a more elaborate recipe for good design. As its name implies, human-centered design is ultra-empathic, but it also misses some important things that are key to wholly empathic design solutions.

An example is the rise and dramatic fall of General Motors' Hummer business. In 2005, you couldn't go anywhere without seeing Hummers all over the road. They were cruising down the freeway above the other cars, stretched versions ferrying prom dates and rappers to and from parties, and they were militarizing the suburban combat theater of supermarket parking lots and drive-through windows.

Why did the Hummer become so popular? In essence, it was because human-centered design was working well. General Motors capitalized on the demand of a specific audience who were clamoring for bigger, more visually powerful vehicles. The United States was coming out of two wars, and a segment of the population was looking to park some of its patriotic fervor in their own driveway.

GM capitalized on this desire with the Hummer. The Hummer driver wanted to sit high and see the road from a powerful, in-command vantage point, and the vehicle was designed to provide that.

But the company mistook its human-centered insights as static versus variable. General Motors assumed that what had been true at one time would be true forever, and it didn't take into account other factors coming out of those two wars. First, the United States entered a recession, and gas prices soared to an all-time high. As the economy worsened, with massive job losses and the shuttering of many businesses from Main Street to Wall Street, many drivers turned against the gas-guzzling monsters.

That alone would probably have been survivable. The company could have taken a knock on the chin and managed through the recession. But it wasn't being dealt a single blow; it was a one-two punch that ultimately knocked it out.

The second, and arguably more powerful, shot was something brewing in the national consciousness, and it had an unlikely hero: the Toyota Prius. That was the US auto industry's first hybrid electric mass-market vehicle, and it brought about an immediate shift in the marketplace.

I don't want to suggest that the Hummer and Prius were fighting for the same consumer. But the Prius brought about a shift in the cultural zeitgeist to a new era of eco-consciousness and consideration for the planet. Electric vehicle (EV) parking spaces started showing up, and owners of those vehicles were given special HOV-lane exceptions. All of a sudden, driving a Hummer became a sort of scarlet letter denoting environmental carelessness. And that—coupled with the downward-spiraling economy and high gas prices—ultimately led to the Hummer's demise.

Hummer wasn't changing to accommodate the new ecosystem, and, as a result, it couldn't survive. If the company had introduced a hybrid model, could it have been saved? Maybe. It did invest briefly in a third-party company called Raser as an attempt to bring electric technology into the business, but ultimately it was too late, and in 2010 GM discontinued the brand.

This is an example of the importance of balancing the influences of ecosystemic versus solely human-centered perspectives in decision-making.

A Bigger World

Empathy with the end user is important—and is perhaps the *most* important thing for meeting consumer demand. But it's not the only thing. Empathy extends beyond the one-to-one interactions we have. We also must consider the one-to-many inputs that empathy helps us to capture.

Do we truly know what's happening in the broader ecosystem? Do we know what our competitors are thinking or doing differently? Are we current with important trends and behaviors the world around us cares about? Staying with the auto industry for another example, the nimble, insight-led company Tesla has capitalized on its understanding of the whole ecosystem to become one of the highest-market-cap automotive brands in the world with only a fraction of the total sales of its next biggest competitors.

It didn't make and sell more cars than the next guy. Tesla became a success by seeing a world that is bigger than car sales and leases. It sees itself as a mobility company that is helping to write the future of the industry. Everyone from consumers to financial analysts understands that that's what it's doing, and it has been rewarded commensurately.

Having a sense of the ecosystem within which our business operates is sure to broaden our perspective and ultimately help its leaders create solutions that stand up to the shifting tides, building more resilient and empathic solutions that meet the needs of those we are trying to connect with more fully.

PASSIVE VERSUS PROACTIVE LEADERSHIP

Gathering information to help make better and more empathic decisions is critical, but there are times when too much is too much. As mentioned earlier, the pursuit of empathy can sometimes lead to analysis paralysis. We can find ourselves in a situation where we have loads of data, sometimes conflicting, and then we cannot act. We're stuck. When that happens, we face the tension of passive versus proactive leadership.

In our work with clients, we take into account diverse forms of feedback: How do they solicit and evaluate the information from differentiated audiences, such as employees, customers, shareholders, and what do they do with the information?

In some organizations, this information-gathering process is done as a matter of process and habit. They capture information, and it goes into a digital repository, never to be analyzed or considered again. It's a strange behavior and more common than you would think.

Now that technology has enabled us to scrape, gather, accumulate, and otherwise parse information from so many sources, many organizations effectively create virtual catacombs housing the specters of consumers past. This happens for many reasons. The most common occurs when an organization's management team knows they need the data or believes they should collect it as a "best practice," but often, the company is not equipped with the right team to analyze it and make it truly useful. So the questions become:

- How much is too much?
- How can companies determine the right level of information to consider before making a decision?
- What is the data informing, and how does that influence leadership decisions?

Some leaders are great at knowing what to do. Decisions come swiftly and often. Deadline-driven businesses seem to excel at it. Go inside any major news organization, and you'll see decisions made swiftly about what to report and how much emphasis to put on a specific topic or story. The Internet turned journalism into a minute-to-minute, twenty-four-hour business, and editors have to make quick choices to stay in front of the competition. The most empathic ones understand their audiences and know what stories will get the most engagement. And engagement grows readership, which draws advertisers and increases revenue. It's a fast-paced, high-intensity business category that must rely heavily on empathy for its audience to make the right choices and drive growth.

Whenever we work with a client to help its team improve their approach to empathy, we first want to understand how they make decisions. We want to know if decisions are being made with adequate, empathic inputs (i.e., inputs beyond those of the decision makers themselves) or in a (relative) vacuum. Equally important, we determine if company or departmental decisions are readily adopted or met with resistance and tension. We want to understand if decisions are made uniformly across the company or if certain groups are better or worse at making decisions that stick. The answers to all these questions help us develop an understanding of the culture at the present moment.

Looking at "Consideration"

Before we can help companies improve their decision-making, we must understand what data and insights they receive in advance of a decision and how they evaluate it. This is the nature of "consideration." Ask yourself: How often do you consider multiple forms of information when making a decision? Leaders must understand this about themselves. We don't all operate the same way, and some people like to take in lots of inputs—customer data, anecdotal insights, conversations with key team members—before making a decision. If that's your leadership style and it works for you and your organization, that's great. But some people get stuck in a loop of too much conflicting information, and it prevents them from taking any real action.

We try to help those people understand and focus on what's most important to consider. Often, they don't need *all* the feedback, just some of it—and delivered in the right format. If a person is a visual thinker, perhaps a word cloud or a chart of some kind will help show the themes or trends more effectively. More verbal leaders prefer to hear or read sound bites from interviews or quotes from key stakeholders to acquire the information they need to make a decision. Every leader needs to have an understanding of his or her unique makeup and how he or she processes feedback.

I'm a visual thinker. I elicit feedback from my team via brief notes or visual references, depending on the kind of decision we are making. All of these inputs are laid out on a table, and I do what's often referred to as a "silent sort." I move things around the table, seeing connections or similarities. I start to notice themes emerge. New perspectives or gaps in the thinking start to become clear. This creates a foundation from which I can make a decision that is informed by collaboration but not overwhelmed by input.

Once you determine the right format, purpose, and depth of feedback that works for you, you'll be in a much better position to make choices.

Proactive Leadership

One thing we tell leaders of organizations is that *all* of their choices have consequences. Every decision a person in power makes will have an impact on the company. It's hard to believe that something seemingly as small as changing the snacks in your break room or the gender identification policies for your restrooms can cause a massive reaction, but that's often the case. Equally, inaction and a lack of decision-making on certain topics can have just as strong an effect.

An organization I've gotten to know over the years is Bridgewater Associates, one of the world's biggest and most respected hedge funds. It is led by a brilliant and enigmatic CEO, Ray Dalio. Ray's vision for Bridgewater is built on the idea of radical transparency—and radical it certainly is.

Ray believes that companies operate most effectively when

everything the company does—from its weekly meetings to the amount of time spent emailing—is made visible to managers and employees. To him, this enables information to be gathered and considered more quickly, leading to more effective and sounder decisions. The results of his hedge fund are hard to argue with, but there aren't too many companies trying to replicate the systems he has in place. I was in the audience at his 2017 TED Talk in Vancouver, where he went into detail about one piece of his radical transparency. It definitely divided the audience.

The controversy was around what Ray described as a custom-designed rating system that runs all day on the computer of every Bridgewater employee. Every interaction, from conference calls to in-person meetings, is graded by everyone who participates. For instance, every employee ranks colleagues in real time, stating whether or not he or she felt the colleague communicated clearly and whether or not he or she seemed effective. These and a slew of other ratings are shared with everyone else, making the transparency immediate and unfiltered.

These data points are fed into one of Bridgewater's proprietary algorithms, which are designed to cross-reference the data with the employee's track record of success, ultimately creating a sort of weighted average of "believability" for each person who works there. When the company is faced with a decision, those ratings can play a key role.

For example, ten Bridgewater colleagues might be discussing a potential stock investment opportunity. They might be at various levels of seniority, but each person's opinion is valued or they wouldn't be in the room. Seven of them are adamantly against investing in the stock; they think the market is too volatile and hard to predict. But three others think Bridgewater should make a big bet on the stock.

If all of their opinions are valued, the decision should be a no-brainer: seven out of ten experts vote against investing, and that's that. But this is where Bridgewater's algorithm comes into play. The algorithm has analyzed a lot of data on the ten employees making the decision—how their investments have performed over time, their effectiveness as communicators, their performance in group decisions versus autonomous decisions—and crunched together a rating for each of them. Of the ten employees, the seven who are against investing were right 36 percent of the time when voting as a group, but the three who want to invest were right 82 percent of the time. As a result, the group will make the investment. Bridgewater uses this sort of data every day to help its teams make more efficient and better-informed decisions about nearly everything.

Some people at TED found Bridgewater's approach to transparency scary and uncomfortable, while others thought it was progressive and refreshing. It would certainly be hard to imagine implementing this type of transparency in all companies.

We can't all rely on Ray Dalio's algorithm (though you can read more in his book *Principles*), but what is this if not empathy? It allows Bridgewater to evaluate decisions from a variety of perspectives. It takes a diverse set of inputs broader than itself and calculates a right decision based on the highest number of knowable details. As we consider situations, we have to account for as many sources as possible, without overwhelming our ability to make informed and meaningful decisions.

Sometimes careful planning can keep us from making bad decisions that would cascade throughout the organization. But sometimes the wrong decision is still made, and when that occurs, it's important to keep feedback channels (verbal and nonverbal) open so that decision makers have the best possible information.

It's not likely that all decisions will be 100 percent correct for everyone, but with a meaningful consideration of inputs into a decision, the best, most empathic solutions can be discovered and acted upon.

THE TIP OF THE ICEBERG

As you apply empathy to your own business practices and teams, you may discover that tensions other than these four will emerge. Inevitably, your success or failure in taking an empathic approach to leadership will rely heavily on your ability to shift the people, processes, and principles of the company to align more fully with the newfound perspective that empathy has given you.

The world's longest-lasting institutions are not businesses but religions, governments, and military forces. They generally succeed because they have the benefit of autocratically dictating the environment in which they operate. Businesses, on the other hand, have to operate within the context of the rapidly changing world around them. If a company cannot continually evolve at the pace of the world around it, it will surely fail.

CHAPTER FOUR EXERCISES

— Exploring the Four Tensions —

These exercises, in the form of questions to answer, will help you calibrate where your company or organization fits on the spectrum of the four common tensions that arise as we begin to apply empathy in our lives and workplaces.

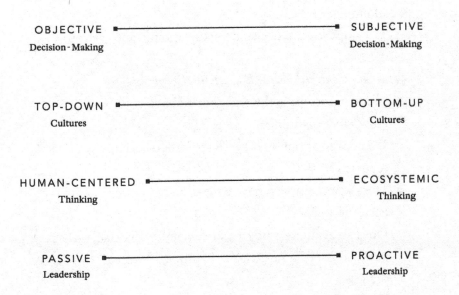

| OBJECTIVE | SUBJECTIVE |
| Decision-Making | Decision-Making |

| TOP-DOWN | BOTTOM-UP |
| Cultures | Cultures |

| HUMAN-CENTERED | ECOSYSTEMIC |
| Thinking | Thinking |

| PASSIVE | PROACTIVE |
| Leadership | Leadership |

Objective Versus Subjective Decision-Making
- What is your organization's comfort with ambiguity?
- How often are facts and data used to inform decisions?
- Is creativity a central part of your company's DNA?
- How is personal and company-wide success measured?
- How much is experimentation tolerated or encouraged?

Top-Down Versus Bottom-Up Cultures
- Is your company's culture democratic or dictatorial?
- Do you have existing structures or policies in place to solicit teamwide feedback?
- How clearly is the company's organizational and reporting structure articulated?
- Do you interact with a relatively narrow or diverse set of employees?
- How quickly are decisions made and put into action?

Human-Centered Versus Ecosystemic Thinking
- How important is the end consumer to your company's planning?
- Do conversations about industry trends occur regularly?
- Does your company have a clear understanding of its customer(s)?
- Does an awareness of greater societal, economic, or political issues figure into the company's thought process?
- What is the most important external factor considered when developing your company's products or services?

Passive Versus Proactive Leadership
- What sort of leadership do you bring to the table with your colleagues? Your department? Your organization?
- How is feedback used as part of personal development at your company?
- When and why do company employees receive communication from senior leadership?
- Does the overall organization consider individual employee growth to be important?
- In your organization, is leadership assigned, earned, or both?

Each of these questions provides only a small window into a company. But evaluated collectively, they will help you uncover the tendencies, deficiencies, and proclivities that have defined the current nature of your business.

Companies seeking to bring more empathy into their culture will need to understand where they stand on the spectrum of these tensions and how that position may accommodate or hinder their ability to include empathic methods.

An acute awareness of these tensions and how to work with them will help make your leadership increasingly more effective.

CHAPTER FIVE

Timeless Empathy

"We've lost our way."

I've heard this from clients countless times. And it's no wonder people are saying this: today's businesses have to evolve very quickly because employees rarely stay in one job for their whole careers and technology is growing so fast that it's a constant battle to keep up with the next new thing.

The stress can be overwhelming. I went through it myself at a time before Sub Rosa was what it is today. That was in 2009, and we were still discovering ourselves and figuring out who we were. It was a brutal time for me. I was twenty-nine years old, recently married, recently split from my business partners, and recently acquainting myself with some negative coping mechanisms in the form of drugs and alcohol. I was mismanaging the tension of running a business, and I was spreading myself too thin.

I'd wake up in the morning hungover from the night before and instantly feeling overwhelmed by everything coming at me at work. I'd drink a lot of coffee to quell the hangover and then amble into the studio and start tackling the problems of the day. My time was split among finding new clients, directing our design team, reviewing the business's financials, motivating a bunch of colleagues who were also at various stages of burnout, and generally keeping myself from drowning.

At the end of the day, I'd head out to get a drink—or many, as was often the case—followed by whatever else might numb me enough to fall asleep. Then I'd wake up and start all over again.

As mentioned earlier in chapter 1, one day it all caught up to me. I was in the studio, and the jug on the water cooler was empty. I bent down to pick up a new one and swung it onto the top of the cooler. In an instant, I saw a white flash of light, and my back crumbled. I fell to the floor, dropping the jug, and gallons of water glugged onto me.

People came running over to see what had happened. They picked up the bottle, which had already soaked me, and they tried to help me up. I was writhing in pain but managed with assistance to hobble to my desk, where I was able to catch my breath and get my wits about me. What had just happened?

Once I calmed down a little, my first thought wasn't to see a doctor but to get back to work. I actually asked for someone to go out to get a cane so I could just keep plodding on. Eventually, someone convinced me to try to take care of my back.

I didn't want to go to the hospital because I was convinced that all would be better in the morning after some rest. Walking slowly with my new cane, I made it home (an eight-block walk) in just under an hour.

The next morning the pain was worse, and I finally gave in and went to the hospital, which led to visits from a group of doctors specializing in back issues. It turned out that I had herniated three discs in my lumbar spine. I was given muscle relaxants and a prescription for physical therapy. I got the full Monty. I took everything Western medicine would give me in the hope of fixing my problem. And each week as I returned to the doctor, the talk turned increasingly to surgery. The docs were convinced that degenerated discs were the cause of my pain, and surgery was their solution.

I had returned to work a few days after the accident, and the stress of that compounded by the constant back pain was destroying me. I was awake all night, unless I combined a couple of drinks too many with pain pills that would dull me enough that I'd fall asleep and flail through nightmares and stress dreams until the morning.

I still put on a positive face and went through each day with as much commitment, leadership, and dedication as I could muster. But the company was rudderless, due in large part to my strained physical and emotional state. I had lost my way, and I was desperate to get the company back on track.

For years, I had heard murmurings about the benefits of Eastern medicine but had never pursued it myself. Now seemed as good a time as any to do so, and I took the advice of a friend and went to see his acupuncturist. Dr. Tsoi Nam Chan's office was near the United Nations and a decent hike from my downtown life. But I had been told he was one of the best, so I made the effort. I walked into his office and was immediately struck by how different it was from the other medical offices I'd visited lately. Not only was incense burning, but the room was filled with beautiful Asian antiques, jade statues, crystals, and meditation fountains. *Where the hell was I, and what was about to happen?*

My immediate impression of Dr. Chan was that he had X-ray vision. He first took a long look at me while holding on to my wrists (which I later found out is a key aspect of Chinese medicine's patient assessment). He made me stick out my tongue (another diagnostic technique of Chinese medicine). He could tell I was majorly exhausted, which had caused a ton of wires to become crossed in my system. He said my back had given out because I had been unable to process the metaphorical weight that I had put on my shoulders. I knew that what he was telling me was exactly right.

Soon I was in a room lying on a table and needles were being stuck into all sorts of odd places on my body. Some were connected to an electric muscle stimulator machine, and electricity was shooting through them and into my muscles to create controlled spasms. I slipped into the most blissful sleep I had had in months.

I walked outside an hour later feeling entirely different. I still had pain in my back, but something had shifted. I felt connected to my body again. I knew this was what I needed if I hoped to fix my back—as well as, perhaps, the rest of my life.

When I got home, I canceled my physical therapy appointments. The PT was helping me repair and strengthen my muscles, but I had now realized I couldn't address my pain on a physical level until I had helped my energetic and spiritual being. And before I could do that, I would have to give my system a break from the drugs and alcohol I was using to numb the pain, help me sleep, help me focus, and help with whatever else I believed they were "helping."

I don't want to give the impression that I'm against Western medicine. I'm a big supporter of what it does for people. But at that moment it wasn't working for me.

I kept up my visits to Dr. Chan, and after a few months of acupuncture, plus a specific concoction of Chinese herbs that would rebalance my imbalanced internal system, I was really starting to feel different. The next step to healing was working on how to better manage the stress I was continuing to endure as a young entrepreneur. I had tried meditation a few times but had found it uncomfortable to sit still because my mind and body were so restless. Dr. Chan suggested that I try tai chi, a Chinese form of moving meditation.

I asked him, "You mean I don't have to sit to meditate?" He smiled and told me no.

The next day I was talking to a friend, and without his knowing about my conversation with Dr. Chan, he told me he had been thinking about learning tai chi. I was blown away by the coincidence. It was a sign!

I set out to find a tai chi teacher (and learned that they are called masters). Later that week I was headed to a friend's holiday party being held in the basement of an Italian restaurant in Brooklyn. I walked down the narrow steps into a sea of people who were standing around drinking wine and eating appetizers. Through the crowd, a small, bald head was weaving its way toward me. Finally, a smiling Chinese man emerged from the crowd and thrust out his hand to meet me. He said, "Hi, I'm Master Ru. I teach tai chi."

You've got to be kidding me, I thought.

MASTER RU'S INELEGANT HORSE

Master Ru's approach was to teach by doing. He moved, and I mimicked his movements (or at least tried the best I could). He described my early attempts to learn his powerful tradition as the fumblings of an inelegant horse. And as we were training, I kept asking questions, such as "What does this pose do?" and "Why are we moving in this direction?" I love the cerebral aspects of learning, and I wanted to understand everything. But Master Ru didn't want to cloud my mind with language and theory. He would just smile and say, "We talk later, just breathe." He is a great master, and he could tell I was trying too hard to think about what we were doing. He knew how to stop me from distracting myself with too many thoughts.

The other thing that made learning from Master Ru so engaging was that we practiced our tai chi outside, no matter what kind of weather we faced. In New York, we get about ten weeks of great weather a year. The rest is either freezing cold or swelteringly hot. But that didn't matter because we did tai chi in snow up to our knees and we did it in 100 percent humidity. That was part of the meditation Master Ru taught. Over time, I stopped noticing the temperature. We'd be standing in the snow, and I'd be sweating from the amount of *qi* (pronounced "chee") I was cultivating. *Qi* is our life force—the energy that powers us. It was truly awesome to see how much more control I had over my mind and body when I was in that meditative state.

After tai chi, Master Ru took me back to his house, where he performed bodywork on me in a tradition called *qigong*. *Gong* essentially means "working." So *qigong* translates to "working with life force." It's a powerful form of energetic medicine that has helped to heal me and many others. Qigong is practiced in different ways. In Master Ru's apartment he manipulated my energy through touch as well as working around my energetic body. Qigong also has poses (like yoga) and meditative practices, and over time Master Ru taught me to do them along with my tai chi practice. That powerful combination of work turned out to be just the medicine I needed to get my mind, body, and spirit onto the same wavelength.

While I was working to mend myself, Sub Rosa was still evolving, too. As things were changing for the better and I was bringing real clarity to my life, I was also working more efficiently, and I was finding time to mentor the team around me and help them grow. But most important, Sub Rosa's core philosophy was beginning to come into focus. That foundation not only was good for the business but ultimately provided a solid base that had a stabilizing effect on me and my ability to lead.

With my newfound momentum and sense of groundedness, I dove headfirst into my exploration of every form of Eastern and new age healing modalities I could find. In addition to my regular acupuncture sessions with Dr. Chan and my training with Master Ru, I tried shamanic healing, sound healing, aromatherapy, yoga, massage, applied kinesiology, hypnosis, craniosacral therapy, and more. I walked the spiritual buffet line for quite some time, sampling various practices and seeing what worked for me. A lesson I learned at a certain point along the path was that I needed to commit and go deep with one or a few practices. An understanding of the world's spiritual practices is helpful, but the real results, the powerful stuff I was seeking, would come only when I committed myself to a specific practice and went deep with it.

Exploring those practices also widened my appreciation for indigenous wisdom. Many of those traditions are the caretakers of the oldest medicines in the world. I was fascinated to discover the communities and practitioners who had maintained those wisdoms and carried them into the modern world. I decided that whenever possible, I would do whatever I could to support the indigenous communities that have continued to preserve and protect those traditions for thousands of years.

One way I would honor them was to train to become a practitioner of the forms that had helped me to heal.

I realized that in my study I had been "taking" from a broad range of disciplines, and I was grateful to the practitioners who had helped me and had been generous and compassionate in sharing their work. But now I went to those powerful healers, shamans, and practitioners with an even bigger request, humbly asking if they would take me on as an apprentice, as someone who had willingly accepted (and was in many ways living proof) that the body, mind, and spirit can work together to heal.

All of them agreed.

COMING FULL CIRCLE

For the next couple of years, I studied with them, sometimes formally in a regular classlike structure and sometimes informally through conversation and workshops we devised together. I devoured books on esoteric sciences and indigenous practices. I became fully immersed. Along the way I met another powerful teacher named Doña Leova. Doña Leova is a Nahuatl *curandera* (medicine woman) from rural Mexico who took me under her wing as though I were part of her own family. Her practice, known as *limpia* (Spanish for "cleaning"), works with touch, plants, prayer, and often an uncooked egg to help diagnose and remove emotional blocks from the body and spirit. Learning this work from Doña Leova challenged my perspective, as initially it was difficult to understand how rubbing an egg on someone would help him or her heal. But time and again, Doña Leova's work brought people to new states of clarity and peace. Working alongside her, I deepened my own knowledge and, in parallel, increased my appreciation of the power of indigenous medicine and the wisdom keepers who carry this knowledge.

I was spending my nights and weekends going deep into those gossamer worlds while I still spent my days leading a growing company. Life and work were busy, but not distractingly so. Things were becoming balanced, and they were more harmonious. One practice fed the other. I had also not experienced back pain in years.

After studying for almost two years, I felt I was prepared to formally work on others. I'd built up the knowledge and the confidence to do the work. I took a deep breath and sent an email to friends and family, telling them what I had been doing with my nights and weekends and invited anyone who was willing to be one of my first clients.

A few brave souls responded.

I was excited to start this new chapter alongside friends and family who believed in me. Many of them were coming with physical ailments—which was perfectly aligned with my initial training. My teachers had taught me that I should first focus only on the physical body before I even entertained the idea of working on any systemic issues or energetic aspects of the body. After all, if you can't help someone's quad muscles heal, you have no business working on their deeper, more complex internal systems. I had also discovered on the journey that the word *heal* brought with it a ton of baggage. Real healing doesn't come from the practitioner; it comes from you. It comes when you awaken to your whole self and allow your system to repair itself. That is what happened to me, and my teachers taught me that our job is not to heal but to put our patients into a position to heal themselves. It didn't take me long to realize how applicable that is to my work at Sub Rosa: our best work occurs not when we fix everything for our clients but when we empower them with the tools and the clarity to fix their own teams, products, culture, or business.

Soon I had patients coming back for additional treatments; what's more, their pains were disappearing. Their tennis elbows were gone. Arthritic hands had regained their motion. Their lower backs were stronger and more stable. It was really working.

I remember the first time I helped a patient heal his low back pain. It felt like I had come full circle. It was wonderful to know that he was feeling better, but for me it was more powerful just to see how far I'd come myself.

In time, more and more people came, and the issues they brought were deeper: chronic, psychological, and spiritual. And my practice expanded with them.

Today I give about fifteen treatments a week, seeing clients before and after Sub Rosa's business hours, as well as on Saturdays. What's interesting is that I don't see my days divided into two parts. Whether my work is in an office or a treatment room, to me there is a commonality. The ability to be present, to listen to another being, to hear his or her needs and connect through empathy, and to help the person get into a position where he or she can move forward—that's what I do, and that's how Sub Rosa evolved into what it is today.

Life seems to know when we need to be presented with opportunities to discover new paths.

I guess I needed to look under the glugging flow of a spilled water jug to be awakened to this side of myself.

THE POWERFUL LESSONS OF THE PAST

During my journey into alternative medicine, I learned that the indigenous communities from which this thinking originated have endured for so many years primarily because of their sense of, and reverence for, their own histories. This is something many leaders lose in our fast-paced world. And it's the reason we too often find ourselves directionless and without purpose.

Most of the leaders in today's C-suites started their jobs well after their company was founded. For that reason, they sometimes lack a sense of the organization's origin story. This is understandable. Sure, they could read some historical documents or interview employees who have been there from the beginning, but if they weren't actually there and didn't *feel* what it was like to be on the ground floor when a company such as Johnson & Johnson or Apple was getting started, it's difficult to make that up. In addition, they rightly place their primary focus on what they're doing *next*, not on where the company came from. This can be just as true for some founders who are still operating the company, and origin stories can start to drift further and further into the rearview mirror.

I discovered this in our work with General Electric. The most "indigenous" aspect of GE's origin story begins with Thomas Edison, whose powerful and innovative ideas were at the heart of the company's foundation. Edison was a big thinker and a solver of huge problems. He said, "I find out what the world needs. Then I go ahead and try to invent it." That's the GE spirit. But it's not always easy to uphold, nor is it simple to stay focused on that premise.

GE has had some huge growth moments when it worked from this place of inspiration. It has succeeded when it has looked into the world and solved big, complex challenges. When it innovates new forms of energy, medicine, or aviation, the company feels like it's on the right path. Its stock price often rises, its employee retention rate is likely to be higher, and its brand experiences a lift in the public eye. But when it has deviated from its origin story—for example, when it has tried to be a bank or a real estate company, which doesn't possess the underlying spirit of Edison's mission—it has faltered.

Over time, I've seen GE take some of those off-course endeavors and move them back into the right position. The management of GE Capital realized it couldn't be competitive if it simply offered to invest the same way the world's big banks did. Instead, they shifted their position to say, "We're not just bankers, we're builders." The idea was that when GE Capital invested in your business, you weren't just getting funds, you were getting decades of experience running large, often complex manufacturing businesses. Its people came in like a well-trained SWAT team and worked with businesses to create cost savings through energy efficiencies; they retooled factories to be more logistically and operationally sound; they brought their spirit of invention into their holdings, and everything took a turn for the better. In essence, they added a little Edison to the business.

Often the best way we inspire our clients for the future is when we connect them to the most indigenous part of themselves, to understanding why they were founded and why they are still here. The greatest "medicine" is already inside us; sometimes all we need is a little help reconnecting to it.

EMPATHY FOR YOUR OWN ROOTS

Pamela Kraft is what I often describe as a "white witch." I mean this with the utmost respect and admiration. She has a mystical and otherworldly quality that she has cultivated for years and channels it to bring good things into being. She's an esoteric who somehow keeps one foot in this world and another in the beyond. I was introduced to Pam by Gil Barretto; the two of them had been hosting monthly group meetings since the early 1980s. In her youth, Pam was a muse and contemporary of artists such as Andy Warhol and Ray Johnson, and her own art takes many forms. But to me, Pam is a painter of connections, and she supports the people and communities she cares about. She holds space elegantly—she is a true Convener.

Somewhere after her wilder years in the 1960s, Pam became connected to indigenous wisdoms, and it awakened something within her. In 1992, she attended the Rio Earth Summit in Brazil, where she met many indigenous peoples and began her journey to support them. She made a commitment then to dedicate her life to those important communities, and her dedication to them has been unwavering ever since. She started an organization called Tribal Link Foundation, which, in affiliation with the United Nations, works to preserve, protect, and empower indigenous leaders from around the world.

I met and got to know Pam while I was training with Master Ru and beginning my indigenous medicine education with Doña Leova. I also think of Doña Leova as a white witch, for the same affectionate reasons I apply that term to Pam. Both of these powerful women have the gift to use their love and their compassion to perform alchemy. They truly facilitate healing in both our inner and outer worlds. I'm honored to have worked beside both of them for so many years.

It was my training with Doña Leova that showed me how important it was to support and protect indigenous cultures, and that led me to ask Pam how I could help Tribal Link Foundation. Within weeks I'd joined the organization's board, and Pam and I have worked together to help it continue to grow and serve as many communities as possible. That work has helped me form many lifelong relationships with indigenous leaders and elders, from Native American holy men to chiefs of Amazonian tribes. I have been granted an opportunity to hear their stories, to understand more about their traditions, and to see how the foundations of their ancestral communities were built.

I know how crazy it sounds that I was doing all of this while still running Sub Rosa. Just doing one of those things probably seems like a full-time job, never mind doing all of them at once. But we create room for the things that matter in our lives, and all of them mattered to me. My dear wife has been a supportive and loving partner to me throughout it all, and in truth, she has been my most important teacher (and is a powerful white witch herself).

My work with Tribal Link Foundation and the indigenous communities it serves has helped me to empathically connect with some of the elemental parts of these resilient cultures. In so doing, I've discovered that the things that matter to these tribal communities today are things that have had the same level of importance and significance to them for centuries. It became clear that those key elements could, and should, be translated and applied to the business world. They include:

- Origin story: How it all began
- Language: Your shared lexicon
- Traditions: How you engage your community and acknowledge milestones
- Purpose: Your reason for being

Think about it: these are the building blocks of every thriving community. Whether in a tribe, a religion, or a corporation, these four building blocks are what provide meaning and create the connective tissue that forms a lasting foundation from which to grow. It was time to bring this understanding into our practice at Sub Rosa and help our clients connect empathically to their own origins and to discover how those origins can be used to help guide them into a new future.

A TRADITION IN DENIM

The first opportunity to use this thinking came to us almost out of the blue. It began with an email late one afternoon from a friend who said a Levi's executive was passing through New York on his way back to San Francisco. He wanted to meet with firms he wasn't already familiar with because he was looking for help solving a problem with the brand. My friend kindly made an introduction, and two hours later, Erik Joule walked through the door.

Erik is the kind of leader who lights up a room. His energy and *joie de vivre* are contagious. Within minutes, we felt as though we were old friends.

He said Levi's had missed a major opportunity by not participating in the "premium denim boom," and it was now suffering both reputational and financial challenges. The premium denim boom had occurred when a number of high-fashion brands entered the market and began selling $200-plus pairs of jeans. During that time, Levi's had maintained its traditional price point of around $39, and as a result, its jeans had acquired a low-end reputation and were considered less chic and no longer fashionable. The company was experiencing a significant sales slump.

We had been involved in a similar conversation not too long before with Absolut Vodka, whose management felt the company had missed out on the "premium vodka boom." Apparently this premium boom was a phenomenon in a number of sectors. In the 1980s, Absolut was a top-shelf vodka. But in the 1990s, competitive vodka brands such as Grey Goose and Ketel One came onto the market with a more premium-priced product. Absolut, like Levi's, had stuck to its price point and dropped to a midtier status, losing market share to the new entrants. Ultimately Absolut found a way out of this by creating its own specialty, limited-edition lines such as Absolut Brooklyn, created in partnership with Spike Lee, and premium-crafted versions such as Absolut Elyx, which was sourced and distilled in a manner designed to compete with other premium vodkas.

Levi's needed a strategy to help it overcome a similar challenge. Like Absolut, they had slipped to the middle tier of its market after having led it for a long time and even though there had been no changes in its products' quality or distribution.

Erik told us that Levi's had hired Wieden + Kennedy, a well-known and successful advertising agency, to help rejuvenate the brand. It was working on a new campaign that was being kept top secret, but he let us in on it. The campaign, which would later be known as "Go forth," was being shot by a famous fashion photographer, and it would draw on inspirational imagery and language from well-known American authors such as Walt Whitman and Jack Kerouac. It would depict a new era of American nostalgia, and it was sure to capture attention.

Erik repeated this: "It's going to capture attention, but attention isn't going to change our business on its own." He wanted our help in turning that attention into action. Our job was to make sure that once they had people's attention, there would be something to act upon and a real reason to care about the brand.

This is the sort of integrated, complex challenge we love to solve, and we first began by focusing on the brand as we knew it. The company made denim and sold jeans (primarily) at a modest price point. They had once been the jeans of Marlon Brando and Steve McQueen and later the jeans of rock stars from the Rolling Stones to the Ramones. But somehow the company had lost its grip.

We asked what had come before Brando and Jagger. Levi's

had begun making jeans in 1853. What had the company stood for then, and what was its origin story? Our research had begun.

It's fairly common knowledge that Levi Strauss & Company started out as a brand of pioneers. The men who had set out for the gold hiding in the uncharted lands of California during the famous Gold Rush of 1849 were known as the 49ers, and they had taken a big gamble, often risking life or death, to try to strike it rich. Those tough men needed tough jeans, and that's what Levi Strauss produced. They had reinforced stitches and held up during hard work. Over the coming decades, Levi's rugged jeans continued to be a staple of the hardscrabble masses. Factory workers, laborers, farmers, and all manner of builders and fixers wore Levi's as they headed out to work. They were the jeans that helped build America.

We had to tell the story in a way that would ignite a new-found interest in the hearts and minds of new consumers and (hopefully) would bring back some customers the brand had lost along the way.

PANNING FOR GOLD

We asked ourselves, "Who are our modern-day pioneers?" After all, we're not settling the West anymore, and many hard-labor jobs have since been shipped overseas. We wanted to find people who were embodying that spirit of progress and hard work and pull them into a new conversation, one that celebrated their sense of craft, of making things, of the integrity that comes from doing that kind of work well.

After a few weeks of development, we had created a program we called Levi's Workshops and sent it off to Erik and his team. We admitted that what we were giving them was "only 75 percent of the plan." The rest would have to be left open to serendipity. We knew we were going into the unknown, like the gold panners of the nineteenth century, and similarly we knew something about what we'd find but not everything. Like any good prospector, we knew to leave room for the unexpected. After all, you never know where you might strike it rich.

A few days later, Erik let us know that the Levi's Workshops had been discussed internally and the team was interested in moving forward. We were a go!

Together, our two teams became one unit. It didn't take long for us to develop a working and speaking lingo, a kind of shorthand. When we said "pioneer," we weren't thinking of a grizzled old prospector chewing tobacco and swilling whiskey, we were imagining today's artists, craftspeople, designers, teachers, and builders. When we said, "Go forth," we knew we were looking for the spirit of adventure and discovery we wanted people to feel when they interacted with the brand. This shared language was built upon the origins of the brand, yet it was contemporized and translated for today. It drew our own teams closer together and became contagious throughout Levi's organization.

Within months we were ready to open our first Levi's Workshop in the heart of San Francisco's Mission District, which was chosen because the neighborhood was thriving with diversity and craft. It felt like a pioneer town for new ideas. Upstart businesses were opening alongside neighborhood strongholds, living and working together with the same spirit inside each of them.

The project had a small-scale urban renewal vibe. We were able to rent an abandoned laundromat on Valencia Street for a dollar because the building's owner knew how much money we would have to invest just to revive the space and make it usable. Our COO, Jeff, still says we overpaid.

We wanted every Levi's Workshop to house the equipment needed to perform a specific type of craft, and our goal was to encourage people to come off the street and join trained craftspeople who could help them roll up their sleeves and make something. They didn't need any prior experience; they just needed the will to "Go forth" and try something new—to be a pioneer, to take a risk and see where it might lead.

We centered that first workshop around San Francisco's long history of printmaking and brought in vintage printing presses. We had letterpress and screen-printing stations. We had poster-making classes and T-shirts you could screen with anything you'd like. Soon we had people lining up to try their hand at all of the amazing tools, and more important, we had people waking up to the idea that they could try something new without being self-conscious about failing.

Scattered among the printmaking materials were a few select pieces of Levi's product. Selling jeans wasn't the workshop's primary purpose, but we wanted people to know that everything was being brought to them, free of charge, by Levi's. We also filled the space with interesting programming that was designed to engage with different communities around San Francisco.

The programming was built on collaborations with "pioneers" from the Bay Area. Right down the street from us, the writer Dave Eggers had opened his first whimsical tutoring location (themed as a pirate shop), where volunteers taught kids the value of creative writing. We partnered with them and paired the kids' writing with artists who created original artwork for their stories. The kids got to watch the books being printed in the shop, and they were dazzled as they flipped through a book that had come to life from their story.

We brought in Alice Waters, a pioneer of California cuisine, and designed a beautiful letterpress harvest calendar that supported the work of her charity, the Edible Schoolyard Project. She hosted a small dinner in the space and signed copies for us to sell at auction, with the proceeds benefiting her cause as well as the Levi Strauss Foundation, the company's charitable organization.

Not only did each project bring into the workshop a compelling pioneer to help create programming, but every piece of programming was designed to reach different subcultures and niche audiences in the Bay Area with authenticity. These new traditions we were creating for the brand were building on Levi's legacy of engaging with powerful subcultures. From gold-panning pioneers to punks on the Bowery, Levi's has always been the uniform of the brave and status quo challenging. We built programming for the literary community, musicians, foodies, inner-city youths, and more. If you were willing to "Go forth" and try something different, we wanted you to know that Levi's was with you.

One of the collaborators we worked with helped fulfill a childhood dream of mine: making my own baseball cards. Growing up, I had collected the cards of all my favorite players. I'd memorize their stats, storing their on-field successes in my memory to be recited later around the lunch table with my friends. But for the workshops we decided to celebrate a different side of the sport. We collaborated with the San Francisco Giants and Topps, an iconic baseball card manufacturer, to design and print a set of cards that praised the off-field accomplishments of San Francisco's athletes. The cards honored the charities they had started and the communities where they volunteered. We made those on-field heroes even larger than life, showing that they were doing more than just winning on the field, that they were branching off from their day jobs to create positive change in their communities. That culminated in a Levi's Night at AT&T Park, the Giants' home field, where cards were handed out to every ticket holder. It was a magical thing to witness.

As the workshop began to take off, we realized that we were creating a new sense of purpose. The Levi's executives were coming into the space and seeing how electrified people were, and that excitement was contagious. The brand was on people's lips again. People understood what it meant to "Go forth" and do something brave and different. A connection to the brand's most indigenous roots was breathing new life into it. We might not have been resettling the West, but we were on a new frontier.

As our time at the print workshop was coming to a close, our clients called to approve us to do another one. The Levi's Workshop was going to New York!

A few months later, we were up and running in downtown Manhattan, this time focused on photography. New York's long tradition with this art form gave us a fantastic palette from which to paint our collaborations. We had photojournalists and fashion photographers join arms with other collaborators to follow the work we had done in San Francisco. At the same time, we continued to hold true to our tradition of serendipity. And we weren't disappointed.

One day, Michael Stipe from the band R.E.M. came into the photo workshop. He had just been walking past and was curious. He poked his head inside and asked what was going on. One of our staffers explained what the shop was, and Stipe asked if he could do a photo shoot in the space. Our staff was quick to say yes, and we were even able to work with his request to do a shoot right then. Thankfully, in the early days of building the workshops we had prepared ourselves to be opportunistic should something like this occur. We had "planned for serendipity," the best we could, eager to capitalize on whatever opportunities might come our way.

Before we knew it, Stipe was on Twitter calling for volunteers to get involved. Within an hour, there was a line of people wrapped around the building who had heeded Stipe's call. He saw more than two hundred people and picked fifty to stay to do a series of time-lapse portraits set to music he had already recorded. At some point in the night, he bought pizzas for everyone who'd stayed to make the crazy project happen. The next morning the video was live on R.E.M.'s website and was being talked about in the news as the latest project to come out of the famed Levi's Workshop.

"Pioneers" were lining up to "go forth." It was exciting to see this brand's origin story come alive in this new and modern way. The project finished its New York run, and we headed off to Los Angeles, where naturally, the theme was filmmaking. Again traditions were played back to the community. We had events that celebrated local "pioneers," charitable programs that gave back to the local community, a constant celebration of craft that permeated our four-month stay at the workshop's home at the Museum of Contemporary Art, offering a variety of classes, activities, and programs.

At the end of 2011, Levi's chief marketing officer, Doug Sweeny, held an all-hands meeting of the internal and external partners involved in the brand. We had spent a wild year building the program, but we were only a slice of the "Go forth" pie. There were tons of digital campaigns as well as big mass-media advertising that was running everywhere to drive attention toward the brand. When he started by saying the brand was back, the room erupted in applause. It was something all of us had worked hard to hear, and together we were responsible for the success.

A few minutes later, he put up a slide with the Levi's Workshops logo. I got the chills, and I had no idea what he was going to say about our work. I knew we had delivered what the client wanted, and in some ways, we had even exceeded its expectations. But it was still a nerve-racking moment. He said the Levi's Workshops had helped the brand come back to its roots and celebrate everything the business had been built upon. He said the Levi's Workshops weren't just something the brand "did" that year but something the brand "does." But the biggest surprise for me was when he announced plans to roll out workshops in major international markets in the following year.

Levi's Workshops went up in Mumbai, Paris, Rio, and other markets where the brand needed to connect to the local community and tell the story of its roots. The program did something special: through actions, not words, it showed people where the brand came from and where it was going. But it also delivered major business results. We tracked billions of earned media impressions, marketing-speak for eyeballs on the brand. Levi's was back in the cultural consciousness in a big way with coverage in virtually every major news outlet. Sales were up, too. Though it would be difficult for us to take all the credit for that, there was undoubtedly a knock-on effect from all of our work helping to drive new sales for the brand.

Our work with Levi's showed us the value of looking back to a brand's indigenous roots and bringing thoughtful inspiration and wisdom into the present. Admittedly not every company has a brand that is more than a hundred years old, but every business does have an origin story.

CONNECTING WITH YOUR ORIGIN STORY

If your company's founder is still alive, find a way to connect with him or her. Understand why he or she started the business in the first place. What was the point? You might be surprised to hear that this person has a different story than the one you were told in your HR orientation. But the origins of your business don't have to stop there. Use this as an opportunity to question convention and challenge the language and the traditions you see your organization using. Make sure that they are actually true to the company's legacy and are being used in the right way. So much of maintaining an empathic connection to our past involves its stewardship in the present. Sometimes things can get a little muddy.

I've observed so many companies that have gotten lost in their own jargon—bandying about staid buzzwords such as "innovation" and "disruption" alongside idiosyncratic acronyms that have meaning to only a few people in the company. One day I looked out our window and saw a truck outside that actually said, "Innovation in Ice." *Are you kidding me?* I thought. *It's frozen water. It's been frozen water forever. What are you innovating?*

CANONIZING THE RIGHT THINGS

Sometimes companies fail to capture the real parts of their origins and the wrong things get carried forward. I remember being taught that lesson in a business course I took in college. The case focused on a multinational company that had a policy of issuing checks only every other Tuesday. The company was engaged in thousands of daily transactions, and that policy was causing them to run up outrageous sums in late-payment fees. The policy had been used in the business from its beginnings, and it had been accepted unquestioningly for decades. But finally an outside consultant was brought in to look at all aspects of the business and discovered that in the company's early days, they had a part-time bookkeeper who worked only every other Tuesday. That little detail had solidified into an unchecked and dysfunctional policy that was hurting the daily operations of a global company.

Instead of being trapped in this sort of rut, ask yourself what you can do to change the lexicon or ingrained behaviors that are keeping you, your team, or your company from growing and align it back to the origins of the brand. Not *everything* is canon, and sometimes the wrong things are treated with reverence. To truly connect with the roots of our brands and businesses, it is important to scrutinize and determine what is core—the most essential—to who we are and what we do.

At Sub Rosa, we talk about this as brand "indigeneity." We have certain words and phrases we have used for years, and they are aligned and consistent with the business we've built. The archetypes are a perfect example of this. We use them as a sort of shibboleth, a shorthand inside language that is unique to us. To us, they're part of our canon.

We also have traditions that keep us focused on what really matters. One of those traditions is something we call our "fresh eyes" meeting. Every few months we gather all of the newest people to the Sub Rosa family for a roundtable conversation with a few of the senior leaders in the company. We call the session "fresh eyes" because the new employees still have the benefit of some objectivity, some external perspective on things. That perspective doesn't last forever, so we take this opportunity to ask them what they see that we do well, what we could do better, what's confusing, and what's refreshing. Who knows? We might be overlooking something important such as the check-writing-every-other-Tuesday example. It's a great tradition we've developed that continues to give us a fresh view on our business.

Before you can manifest your company's purpose, you need to know what it is, and it needs to be uniformly understood across the company. For years, we have been consistent in our language and our purpose, and every member of our team internalizes them and brings them forth in their work. In its simplest form, Sub Rosa helps companies explore, learn, and grow with empathy. This is our root structure, our foundation. It's that strong connection to our origins that creates a powerful path to understanding where we've come from and, ultimately, how we'll arrive at our next destination.

CHAPTER FIVE EXERCISES

Connecting to Your Roots

This exercise will help you use this chapter's four-part framework to unearth the powerful elements of a company's early beginnings. They will serve as provocations for articulating what is most indigenous and valuable within your own organization and establishing a strong foundation from which to grow and evolve.

Origin Story

A first step is to commit your company's origin story to written form. If you're the founder of the company, you've got a head start because you probably are a big part of the story. But only a few of us are founders, so if you aren't one, you need to seek that person out, along with other team members who were there during the early days. Remember, you are looking not just for who did what but primarily why the company was started and what drove the founder(s) to bring it to life.

If the founder(s) are not available to you, a good place to start is early documents, such as bylaws, mission statements, letters to the staff, and so on. Treat this exercise like a scavenger hunt for the company's early artifacts. Talk to retired or early-stage team members. Hunt down press articles about the company. Use your empathic, intuitive skills to get into the mind of the founder(s) and develop a sense of the most important aspects of the business; look for the ones that still serve the company and its mission today.

Language

Is there an internal lexicon that the company uses, formally or informally? Do team members speak in a code of acronyms and phrases that are unique to the business? If so, ask yourself why that is and delve into the meaning behind those phrases or terms.

It's likely that the language was established while the company was defining what it is (and is not), and decoding it will reveal more than just meanings of words and phrases. Levi's has talked about pioneers since the Gold Rush, but the term has evolved over time. Today it doesn't refer to the same people as it did more than 150 years ago, but it captures the same idea. What words like this are ingrained in your company's essence, and how can you make them relevant to today's world?

You may find some common "inside baseball" language that isn't connected to the past but has taken root more recently as a result of new leadership or direction. It is also helpful to understand these terms as an insight into the values of the company's culture.

Traditions

For this exercise, start by documenting two to three of your team's or organization's traditions, being sure to include the details of their origins, why the company continues to do them, and what they add to the overall culture of the business.

Next, take a moment to identify your team's or business's current pain points. For instance, what do you unnecessarily endure or struggle with on a regular basis?

Now consider if there is any connection between the traditions you identified and the pain points. Are some traditions actually causing pain in the current business? Are the traditions oblivious to the issues? Or perhaps the traditions could be used better—directing them at the issues you identified to help cure them. Take a moment to outline your thoughts on this topic, and see if an opportunity emerges to use traditions in a new way.

In addition, it's entirely acceptable for companies to create new traditions based on the direction the company is going in.

Ask yourself what sort of new traditions might be created to help change circumstances for the better. Consider some of these thought-starters:

- *Should the tradition be designed to add to or subtract from the issue?* For example, if you have too many pointless meetings, you might consider a monthly tradition of evaluating and editing down all current meetings.
- *Should the tradition be based on your newfound origin story?* Could an aspect of the company's history be reignited in the hearts and minds of the current team?
- *Should the tradition work with your internal team, or would you be better served by creating a tradition that includes an external party?* Consider inviting your customers or clients into the new tradition to help broaden participants' perspectives.

Purpose

The exercises in chapter 3 included a way of using the Aspirational Self to establish and understand your own *raison d'être*, or purpose. Let's now pull out to a wider perspective, no longer considering just yourself but the whole team or organization.

Conduct the same exercise, mapping information into the Venn diagram on the next page and see what you place at the center. This process helps to illuminate the primary purpose of your team or organization and will ultimately aid in making more focused, informed decisions aligned to your overall reason for being.

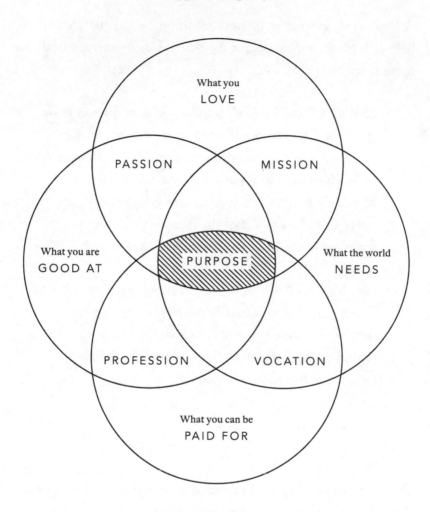

CHAPTER SIX

Our Role in Context

In 2017, my phone's caller ID lit up: "US Government." Immediately I flashed back to every remotely dubious act I've ever committed. Was I sure I'd paid that speeding ticket in New Mexico? Had my college pot dealer's cell phone been seized? I couldn't imagine why the government was calling me.

Cautiously I picked up and was greeted by a pleasant-sounding man who introduced himself. "Hi, Michael, this is Captain Bokmeyer from the United States Military Academy at West Point."

A sigh of relief—I wasn't going to jail (yet).

Captain Justin Bokmeyer was an avid listener to our *Applied Empathy* podcast, a monthly series we had been producing for a little more than a year. He was hoping that Sub Rosa could come to West Point to work with some senior cadets, the coaches in the athletics department, and, if that went well, the generals who run the academy. He wanted us to talk about our philosophy on empathy and help some of the West Point instructors find ways to incorporate it into their training programs.

That was kind of mind blowing. West Point wanted us to help it become more empathic? Perhaps it was narrow-minded of me, but I had never imagined that the military would have a strong desire or demand for empathy. It was too cool an opportunity to pass up. I told Captain Bokmeyer to count us in, and we set a date for a few weeks later.

We do this sort of training often, but typically the audience is more "corporate" or "design" focused. I knew I had better give some thought to how the groups at West Point might hear what we have to say. Would they be skeptical? Would they think applied empathy sounded too "soft" and emotional? I'll admit I even had a brief crisis of confidence when I pictured myself in a room full of military personnel talking about "Sages" and "Seekers." I wondered if I should make changes to my usual presentation, altering some of our language to sound less mystical, but the material had already won over plenty of tough-minded CEOs, so I kept it as is.

EMPATHY ARRIVES AT WEST POINT

A month later, as I drove through the springtime bloom of trees along New Jersey's Palisades Parkway, I was nervous again. I wasn't worried about my material, but this particular assignment had extra significance for me. I have great admiration and respect for the men and women of our armed services. They have chosen a life of service to protect our rights and freedoms, allowing me to live my life talking about branding, practicing indigenous medicine, and writing books. I take what they do seriously, and if this was an opportunity for me to give something back to them, I wanted to do a really good job.

Arriving at the gate, I saw military police checking identification and inspecting vehicles, and that's when another pang of anxiety shot through me. Maybe I was a smuggler in a past life, because inspections like that always send me into a state of fight or flight. After a quick chat with the stone-jawed officer, I was waved through to visitor parking, where I met Captain Bokmeyer and was immediately put at ease by his warm smile and crisp handshake.

His hair was cut short, his eyes focused, and his posture like a board. "Great to meet you, sir," he said confidently. When we'd spoken on the phone, I had already said he didn't need to call me "sir," but I guess old habits die hard. He said we would first head to the athletic facilities, where we would begin empathy training for the coaching staff. It was 7:30 a.m., and the campus was already alive and in motion.

Driving across the historic campus, we passed cadets going through their morning drills while I focused on how I was going to connect empathically with the West Point coaches by putting myself into their shoes. I thought back to the coaches I'd had when I was growing up. Sports were a huge part of my life. I went from basketball to hockey to baseball to pickup games or simply skateboarding around town. My supportive parents, driving me to and from practices, scrimmages, and tournaments—they must have felt as though it were a part-time job.

COACHING EMPATHY

Playing so many sports, I learned early on that some coaches were better than others. But to be fair, that was also true of my own athletic abilities. I quickly took to some sports, such as basketball and track and field, while others, such as soccer and baseball, seemed to have been designed to highlight my lack of coordination. Still I persevered, and many times I discovered that it was the coach who made all the difference in whether or not I improved.

169

I had coaches who barked orders from the sidelines, their faces red while they screamed at preteens as if we were training for the Olympics. I had phone-it-in coaches who ran us through some drills and then collected their paycheck. They had little interest in the win-loss column and were more concerned with not being hassled by parents who wanted to know why their kids weren't playing enough or why practice started late. I also had my own dad, who loved sports and always volunteered to coach whatever youth team I was on. That was a great experience for both of us, but as I grew up and started to play more competitively, he (begrudgingly) moved to the sidelines. In retrospect, I think what I was observing with the best of my coaches was a sense of empathy. But I hadn't seen anything until I met Coach Harry.

In high school, I was a lanky six-foot-tall freshman when I went out for the basketball team, led by Coach Harry. He had something I couldn't quite put my finger on. Some of my teammates got a stern talking-to when they passed the ball sloppily; others were praised when they did something right. His technique with me was different: he pulled me aside and demonstrated, calmly and without condescension, how I could change my footwork to give me a better position on the court or how I could alter the angle of my elbow to improve my shooting. I didn't have the word for it at the time, but what Coach Harry was teaching me—aside from how to hit a ten-foot jump shot—was empathy.

He understood each player's makeup and knew how to adjust his coaching style in ways that would get the most out of all of us. The best coaches, like the best leaders, use empathy to do their job well. They know which players thrive on discipline and which ones need more gentle mentorship. Some of this is intuitive, but I believe they learn it by testing which approach gives them the best results with different kinds of people. I hadn't thought about that for more than two decades, but as we drove across the West Point campus, these memories flooded back and helped give me the confidence to walk into a room filled with fifty accomplished career athletic coaches.

Whether they knew it or not, empathy was already a big part of their coaching arsenal. No professional, college-level coach can get that far without having *some* empathy up his or her sleeve. My job was to help them realize that and to help them connect to it more deeply. We began by discussing the tensions that arise and how empathy can help a coach get through them. I always find it helpful to lay those out early in the conversation so that people recognize that working with empathy will bring out certain challenges. It's a normal part of the process, and my doing this helps people become comfortable enough to proceed.

I then described the Empathic Archetypes. We talked about each one, and I asked the coaches to examine their strengths and weaknesses across each of the seven archetypes. Heads were nodding in the crowd, and many of them took voluminous notes.

One of the coaches asked, "Are you saying we need to pick one of these archetypes and focus only on that as a coaching style?" This was a great opportunity to highlight the flexibility of using the archetypes, and I began by explaining that actually, it's quite the opposite; we want to raise our awareness of all of the different archetypes, recognizing that having a broader array from which to choose helps us get the most out of each person on the team. The coaches liked hearing that because it reinforced something they already intuitively knew: that every player is different and good coaching depends on being able to pivot from one style in order to get the most out of all of them. I gave Coach Harry a little mental fist bump for helping set me up for that conversation.

I walked through a few case studies, showing how we at Sub

Rosa put empathy into action. Then I opened the room for some conversation. I recall a comment from the head football coach. Army football has a long and lasting legacy throughout all of college sports, so I knew that being the head coach at West Point is a big deal. He said, "Coaching is based on instinct and an understanding of the talents and mind-sets of our athletes. Even though we are in a very command-and-control military environment, we as coaches need to remember that we'll get the most out of our players when we approach each of them with a sense of empathy for how they are best motivated." This felt like a huge win for the approach we've been developing over the years.

BASIC (EMPATHY) TRAINING

Later that day I met with several different groups of cadets and ran through a similar series of workshops. When West Point cadets graduate, many of them are deployed as officers in the US Army and immediately made responsible for leading forty soldiers who themselves are just barely out of their teenage years. That's forty lives they must direct and protect. I don't know about you, but I had a hard enough time keeping myself out of trouble at that age. The cadets I saw at West Point believed that understanding how to apply empathy would be useful to them in the next phase of their journey.

We had just begun using the Q&E cards a few months earlier at training sessions to help people "limber up" their empathic muscles, and I had a feeling they would also help the cadets get their minds ready to think more empathically.

Soon after we passed out the cards, I could see the cadets beginning to identify which archetypes matched with their empathic strengths and weaknesses. The conversations among them were about improvements they could make, and they went the next step of drawing cards that corresponded to their least comfortable archetypes and figuring out how they could boost their skills in those areas. As soldiers, they took naturally to training and development, and they dealt with the archetypes easily. After just a few hours, those bright, talented young leaders had begun to make empathy a part of their tool kit. It was an honor to play a role in bringing a new skill to those soldiers at that critical time in their development.

A few days later, Captain Bokmeyer called again. I was beginning to like seeing "US Government" show up on my caller ID. He wanted me to come back, this time to work with the generals of West Point. Soon I found myself in a room full of laser-focused, clear-eyed career military officers. "*This* is going to be a tough room," I thought. Not only was my material a little "new age," but I seriously stood out with my beard and long hair. Still I soldiered on and was happy to discover that they were genuinely interested in delving into empathy training.

We talked about the tensions that arise when we engage with empathy, the Empathic Archetypes, and a few case studies; the same as I had shared with the other groups. Then I distributed the Q&E cards and asked the generals to pair off and ask each other some questions from archetypes they perceived to be strengths and some they felt were potential weaknesses.

Just as the cadets had immediately connected with the Q&E cards, the generals instinctively knew what to do with them. The decks were quickly divvied up, and the generals broke into pairs to start their conversations.

When the cards are being used, I pay attention to the overall changes in the room. Is the volume getting louder as people engage? Are people smiling? Are they gesticulating? Has the energy gotten lighter? In that case, all of the above happened. I was seeing hardened military generals cracking jokes, in some cases, and leaning in to have heart-to-hearts, in others. No matter how many times I've done trainings like this, it still excites me to see the power of empathy at work.

A SOLDIER'S VIEW OF EMPATHY

I listened in on one of the groups and overheard a general talking about how things had changed since he had graduated from West Point. I thought he might start objecting to the sort of training I did or say it felt wrong for the army. Instead he noted that the theater of war had changed. Soldiers no longer fight in rural areas, far away from civilians and the lives of everyday people. "Today we fight our battles in cities," he said, before asking his group, "Are we training the type of soldier who's going to walk down the street of a village in Afghanistan and unempathically ignore everything at play around him or her, or are we training them to see differently?" He gave an example.

"Let's say we have a soldier walking down a main street of a city. You see, in war, there's times when we're fighting the enemy, but there's also downtime where our soldiers are out among the local community. Now let's say they are walking down that street and they see a scared little kid standing outside their parents' market. That kid is looking at this big, foreign, military fatigue–wearing soldier, and they might be scared. They might be confused. They might have no idea who we are and why we are there. Are we training the type of soldier who walks right by and goes on with whatever they're doing, or are we training the type of soldier who will see that kid and stop to think that maybe they can do something to ease their worry or confusion? Are we training a soldier who will take a knee and talk to the kid, and maybe their family, trying to explain why we are there and what we are trying to do to help them? I hope that's the kind of soldier we are training, and I think empathy is at the heart of that."

Since making that visit to West Point, I have told that story many times. It was eye-opening and inspiring to hear that general speak with such earnest and heartfelt perspective.

At the end of the session, West Point's superintendent (the head of the school) spoke to the group and said that empathy should be the number one new skill taught to West Point cadets. Without it, he said, the army cannot know what's happening outside its ranks. "The American people are our clients," he said, "and if we are going to be successful for them, we need to know how they perceive us and our work."

I was packing my bags to leave when another general approached me. Her name was General Cindy Jebb, West Point's dean of the Academic Board. She reached out her hand to shake mine and in doing so, she palmed me a coin. I thanked her for it, and she thanked me for bringing empathy to West Point, smiled, and walked away.

Later, when I asked Captain Bokmeyer about the coin, his eyes lit up, letting me know it was something pretty awesome. He said it was called a "challenge coin" and is given only in recognition of special achievement or appreciation of a visitor. That coin sits proudly on my desk, a reminder that the power of empathy is alive and well in the people who serve bravely for us every day.

PUTTING EMPATHY INTO PRACTICE

Whether you're a decorated military officer, a renowned CEO, or an up-and-coming entrepreneur, our approach to using empathy to solve problems always starts from the same place. The first step in the process uses a framework we call the Empathy Venn (EV) to guide a person or team in gaining perspective on a problem they need to solve. The EV is made up of three circles, each representing one of three "Cs": company, consumers, context.

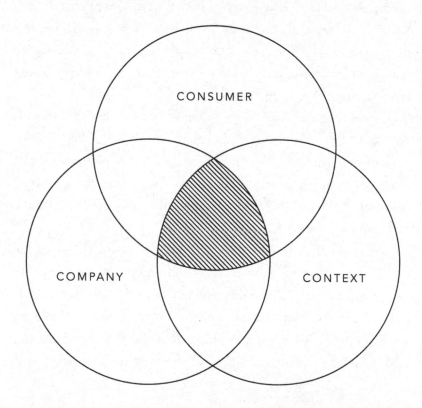

The EV serves as a kind of empathy entry point to start thinking through a particular situation. Once you've used it a couple of times, you'll begin to apply empathy without even having to think about it.

COMPANY

The first step is to examine your company's inner workings. We use the word *company* here, though it could be an organization, as at West Point. We break down the company by considering the following elements. Of course, your business could have other elements and questions, so consider this a starting place for your own exploration.

- *Products and services:* What does your company make or provide to your customers? How many products or services? Why? Do your company's products or services lead the market? If so, why? If not, why not? Have the products evolved over time or remained relatively the same?
- *Team:* Who is at your company? Do the people who work at your company have shared characteristics, skills, or beliefs? If not, how and why are they different? Is the team centralized or decentralized? How do teams work together? Are there processes or behaviors that are unique to your company?
- *Leadership:* How does leadership show up? Is it innate in everyone or limited to a select few? Does your company have clear principles and values? Do those principles and values trickle down into the products and services? Why or why not?
- *Brand:* How does your company talk about itself?

Does it have a distinct point of view? Are its messages clear and differentiated? How does it appear in outward communications such as social media and advertising? What tone do the communications take? Does it have any reputational damage that needs repairing?

- *Behaviors:* What are the commonly recurring terms, actions, and themes that the company espouses? How do they connect to the overall mission?

This list can include additional or different elements depending on the situation you're trying to understand. But the exercise is meant to determine what makes your company tick, why it's unique, how it functions (or doesn't) so that a map can be created that allows you to understand the company in its entirety.

CONSUMERS

We use the word *consumers* to refer to the various audiences relevant to the company. Too often businesses think only of their end consumer, but in addition to those who purchase a company's product or use its service, there may be many additional audiences that consume information about the company. In order to help a company build empathic connections with those audiences, we must have a full picture of who they are. Consider the following.

- *End consumers:* How many end consumers are there? Who are they, and what is their demographic and psychographic makeup? Are they price sensitive? How loyal are they? Why or why not?

- *The media:* What is reported about your company, and who is responsible for disseminating information about the company? Is your company covered in the news regularly? Why or why not? What are some of the common themes?

- *Intermediaries (e.g., wholesalers, retailers, B2B partners):* What role do these groups play? What are their priorities or interests in relation to your company, and how well are they being met? How strong or long-lasting are these relationships?

- *Shareholders:* Is your company private or public? Who has a financial interest in it? Why should people invest in it? How do investors communicate or consume information? At what frequency? Through what channels?

- *Potential employees:* Who seeks employment at your company? How do they find you? Is the information they encounter about your company accurate and consistent with the company's goals? Do you wish to extend beyond this pool of candidates? What other companies do candidates consider, and where can they find information about them?

CONTEXT

Contextual perspective takes into account the ecosystem surrounding a company. For me, this is like a camera pulling way back, seeing a company with a wider, more inclusive lens. It includes the consideration of several factors:

- *Direct competitors:* How do your competitors differentiate themselves from your company? How do they perform relative to your company? What do they see as their competitive advantage?
- *Indirect competitors:* Who is drawing attention or spending away from your company? Why and how? Does your company think of them as a threat? Do they even know they exist? Could alignments with those organizations help your company succeed?
- *Cultural zeitgeist:* What's happening in the world around us? Do any cultural hot topics have meaning for your company? Is that relationship being developed? Why or why not? What are the trends that could upend your company's growth should they not be addressed?
- *Technical trends:* Are new technologies being developed that might enhance or threaten your company's growth? What technologies are consumers currently being drawn to? Do those technologies have a role to play in your company's business? Why or why not?

As you can imagine, this list could easily lead you down a pretty big rabbit hole if it isn't managed carefully. As you expand the lens, more and more things come into view, and we recommend focusing on no more than five to six categories for each of the EV circles.

Once the information for each circle is gathered, connections will emerge. Most important, the shaded part of the diagram, where the circles overlap—and where the three C's connect—is what we call an Empathic Opportunity. This occurs when company, consumer, and context align and each element in the EV is understood. When an Empathic Opportunity emerges, powerful growth can result. For an example of what can happen when this occurs, let's look at the photography company Polaroid.

THE LONG ROAD TO INSTANT SUCCESS

The Polaroid Corporation was founded by Edwin Land in Cambridge, Massachusetts, in 1937 and seemingly overnight became a "juggernaut of innovation," according to the *Boston Globe*. Land was a gifted inventor whose work on products such as polarized sunglasses led to an early version of night vision goggles, which were first used by the army during World War II. The company continued building a culture of innovation over the decades, and then, in 1976, a major breakthrough happened when it figured out how to create "instant film" that would allow customers to see a photograph develop within minutes of taking it. Before long, the company was selling millions of its cameras and film to photographers around the world.

Putting the company through an EV analysis, we can see that its success in 1976 didn't happen overnight. It possessed a culture of innovation dating back to its origins, a reputation in the market that had been developed over time, and a new breakthrough product built on the back of the company's historic growth. Its success with instant film happened at a particular time when it hit a sweet spot in its end consumers' desire for fast, cheaper film processing. That was the 1970s, and the culture was changing at a quicker pace than in previous decades. Every industry was embracing technology, and consumers were responding to each "new" and "next" thing that offered greater speed and efficiency.

The 1970s was a decade when a new consumer with disposable income came of age. The freewheeling hippies who had spent their late teens and early twenties indulging in 1967's Summer of Love were now beginning to start their own families. The baby boomers, who described themselves as "switched on" and living in the "now," were primed to be one of America's biggest and most influential consumer groups. They had a strong desire for "immediacy," and culturally they valued the "present moment." Polaroid offered them a camera that gave them instant mementoes. That's when magic happens—when all three circles have a common intersection point, presenting an empathic opportunity that meets the needs of all three C's.

Polaroid's business spread like wildfire. But the company would eventually learn—to paraphrase the Greek philosopher Heraclitus—that the only thing constant is change.

Over the coming years, the company maintained its focus on two of the three C's. It continued to work on the company as well as the consumers by innovating and developing new products for its film business. But it could be argued that it lost touch with context, when they failed to recognize the massive increase in the use of digital technology and, most important, the emergence of digital camera technology. It's common for market leaders to become so enrapt in their own business, looking toward the next linear move on their growth plan, that they miss a nonlinear tidal wave coming at them from the side.

By the mid-1990s, digital cameras had hit the mainstream, and though Polaroid attempted to compete, it was too little, too late. By 2001, other leaders in the category had taken away Polaroid's market share, and on October 11 that year, the Polaroid Corporation filed for bankruptcy.

How could the Empathy Venn have helped it? When we keep the three C's in focus, we are applying empathy to empower more informed decision-making. It enables us to nurture both the company and our consumers but also helps us maintain a broad aperture on context, which allows us to see the world around us with greater clarity. If Polaroid had used an approach like this, it might have seen clues that digital photography would overtake the film business early enough to have made investments in digital technology, allowing it to provide consumers with the cameras they were now demanding. That approach would have kept the company connected to their founder's origin story, which was centered around innovation.

It's worth noting that since 2001, Polaroid has been resuscitated. In 2009, the brand was relaunched with a new suite of digital and instant film cameras. In 2010, it appointed the musician Lady Gaga as the brand's creative director in a relatively short-lived attempt to capture relevance and audience through her stardom and marketing sense.

Though it's unclear where the brand will go in the years ahead, hopefully the company will draw insights from the lessons of the past and use a more empathic approach. Being informed by the trends of the consumers and context around us help ensure we're not navel-gazing but looking out into the world around us and discovering ways to empathically connect and share our messages, products, services, and purpose more meaningfully.

Building from the Empathy Venn, let's look at what we can do when we've uncovered an opportunity. How can we act upon the point of intersection of company, consumers, and context? It starts with an internal gut check.

EMPATHIC OPPORTUNITY: INTERNAL

Business leaders and brand builders often want to rush out into the world with their product or service, shouting from the hilltops that they have something special that everyone needs to see. But empathic leaders know how to balance that excitement with a sense of rigor, making sure there is a strong connection among company, consumers, and context. The first check of this is an examination of your company's internal workings.

The marketing team of a client in the automotive industry gave us a clear, direct brief that the company wanted to be "known as the most innovative car company in the world." I knew the right thing was to say, "That's great!" letting them know I appreciated their desire to think big and bold. Still I had to ask, "But are you?"

They looked at each other with half smirks. A few rolled their eyes and admitted that their company wasn't the most innovative, but that's what it wanted to be. They'd seen that Tesla, the new darling of the industry, had been growing rapidly, largely on the back of its culture of innovation, and they felt that they, too, should attempt to ride that wave.

We knew we could work with them on some sort of marketing campaign that might grab initial attention, but in the end, it would likely blow up in everyone's faces. The idea was too thin because the company actually wasn't innovative. This highlights an interesting aspect of working with empathy. Often a lack of empathy leads organizations to seek out solutions that don't entirely fit their needs. But they can get so caught up in their own business that they fail to see the bigger picture. Ultimately, applying empathy to our leadership style and our overall business can help us see challenges from new and diverse perspectives.

As our conversations with this team continued, they revealed that they *wanted* to be innovative; they just didn't know where to start. My team and I tried to understand their desire to be innovative and also why they felt it was important to have consumers see the company that way.

What had begun as a marketing conversation evolved into a discussion about the company's internal culture and how a culture of innovation might be created. We talked about how the company's design team might be inspired to think differently about the cars it designed, and we even discussed expanding the company's business beyond the automobile to the more broadly defined area of mobility. That got the team's wheels turning (sometimes the puns are too easy).

In this case, our client had already focused on an Empathic Opportunity—the intersection of company, consumer, and context—through its desire to be seen as innovative. It was time to introduce its team to our internal assessment of the Empathic Opportunity, which examines an organization based on different facets within the company.

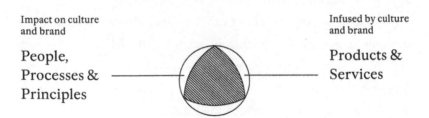

Impact on culture and brand

People, Processes & Principles

Infused by culture and brand

Products & Services

On one side, we look at the internal people, processes, and principles, which greatly determine the company's culture and have an impact on its behavior. It is important to overlay these elements atop the Empathic Opportunity to see if there's a fit or if, as in the case of our auto client, a gap needs filling.

Every major company has something it calls its brand guidelines, brand book, brand bible, or something similar. This is where the company articulates its mission, vision, values, and other core principles. Our automotive client wanted to pursue innovation. That showed up in its brand book, but if the book isn't followed, it's not worth much more than the paper it's printed on.

Our client's gap was in the company's people and processes. It didn't have innovative thinkers who could champion the aspiration for innovation into reality, and it was without an innovation process that would guide thinking, decision-making, and overall behavior toward progress. We took a closer look at the team to help them identify the skills that were missing. Change management doesn't always involve making sweeping layoffs and hiring new people, though sometimes that is necessary. More often it's a balance of bringing in new team members along with thoughtful training and skills development programs. That's what our auto client did. A new design leader was brought in to bring fresh thinking to the automotive design, while employees in other divisions were given skills development training to help them approach challenges with a focus on innovation.

We also helped our client examine its internal processes. We brought in partners from places such as the MIT Media Lab and mobility start-ups to share various styles of working and prototyping. During those conversations, it was surprising to learn that car companies still create clay models of new vehicles before moving them into production. While the craftsmanship to create those models is truly astonishing, we encouraged our client to consider new forms of rapid prototyping such as 3-D printing to help move through design charettes faster.

We also helped the client understand that innovation often requires operational change, but those changes rarely translate into profitability within a quarter or two. It takes time—sometimes years—before innovation yields results. Teams that are evaluated on a quarterly profit-and-loss basis will be reluctant to take bold risks and challenge convention. To change a culture, it can sometimes be necessary to support innovation on a financial and personal performance basis. Our client needed to establish new policies that would give its teams permission to take calculated risks and, at times, accept a loss before obtaining long-term growth.

It's also important to look at a company's products and/or services because they ultimately sustain its culture and behavior. They represent the output of the people, processes, and principles that must meet up with the opportunity. They are the physical manifestation of elements playing well together.

Our auto client's team changed the way they thought about product and, instead of thinking simply about making cars, shifted their focus toward creating mobility solutions. They began to think differently about how people use vehicles in cities versus suburbs and rural areas. And we saw them begin to explore a new set of services, either through new venture creation or investment in existing ventures, which let them play a role in the sharing economy and collaborative consumption business models via carshare programs and other disruptive mobility innovations.

Everything was coming together for that organization, and its people were seeing the benefit of working from an empathic place to act upon their initial instinct to shift into a more innovative culture. With that internal alignment in place, we could begin the work that the client had first come to us to carry out: to tell the world it was an innovator. That company took a big step in the right direction, but empathy and innovation are not magic wands. They take time, dedication, and continuing recommitment to make them a core part of a company's DNA.

EMPATHIC OPPORTUNITY: EXTERNAL

Once we've identified an empathic opportunity and have aligned the company's internal aspects around it, it's time to take the work out into the world. To do this, we bring together a mix of marketing, communications, public relations, sales, customer experience, and media people. But we don't use the traditional "us-versus-them" approach so common in our trade. Instead, we look at the problem through the lens of "we" and use words all of us understand:

- Conversations
- Behaviors
- Relationships
- Memories

This is how Applied Empathy comes to life in the world.

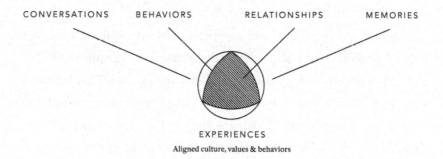

CONVERSATIONS   BEHAVIORS   RELATIONSHIPS   MEMORIES

EXPERIENCES
Aligned culture, values & behaviors

Conversations

The first step any company should take before externally acting on an Empathic Opportunity is to decide clearly and articulately what it wants to communicate. This may seem obvious, but you'd be surprised how often marketers and creative types dive straight into a campaign for a product or service before the company has figured out exactly what it wants to say. The only way to do that empathically is to engage in internal conversations. This goes to the core of the work we do. Building a campaign with empathy begins with asking ourselves:

- What conversation(s) are we trying to have?
- With whom?
- In what channels?
- And most important: Why are we having this conversation?

Asking these questions helps establish the baseline for the company's marketing and communications. We want to understand who we're talking to, how they consume content (e.g., via social media, through advertising), and what we want to say to them once we have their attention.

We worked with a fashion brand that couldn't figure out why its social media following had plateaued. We looked at the content from the past few months and immediately saw that it was overly populated with product-focused content. More than 80 percent of the posts were focused on the latest cuts, styles, colors, and sales related to the product. I asked their communications team, "Imagine if every time we hung out together, all I talked about was my clothes. How often would we hang out?"

They realized in an instant that their communication strategy was too myopic. In their defense, they had been responding to pressure from the company's sales and leadership teams to drive more sales through social media. But together we looked at their audience more empathically and created a plan that could show the leadership that sales wouldn't come from talking about sales.

We looked for other topics for which the brand shared a passion with its consumers, and we landed on music, design, and food. As a test, the media people swapped their sales promotion content for conversations with their followers about their favorite new bands, artists, and restaurants. We helped them think empathically about the consumers they wanted to attract and provide content they knew would interest those consumers.

Within weeks, the company regained its lost audience and began adding new followers to its social media outlets; most important, it established an authentic connection that carried over to its product. Its consumers came to believe that the brand understood them. And guess what? Sales started to rise.

Our work with that client was focused on the conversations the company needed to have because that's where empathy starts. When people connect authentically, bringing about a shared understanding of each other, the greater the likelihood is that everyone will get what they are looking for.

Behaviors

Once your company knows the message it wants to communicate, it is time to determine what behaviors you want to bring about. Sometimes, as with the fashion brand, it will simply be encouraging followership or building a loyal customer base, but it can be a wide range of things, such as:

- Taking a test drive
- Coming to your store and shopping

- Following you on Instagram
- Buying our product

The role empathy plays here is in recognizing that your consumers are savvy, and they know when companies are marketing to them. So it's important that you be clear about your intention, whatever it is. You're not going to pull one over on them. With a clear conversation in hand, you can construct a path toward the desired behavior(s).

Relationships

When your conversations with consumers start eliciting the behaviors you desire, that is the start of a relationship. But, like any relationship, it must be maintained so it continues to grow. How you do that is by applying empathy and anticipating what your consumers want from the relationship. How often do they want to hear from you? Should your communication be personalized at this stage of the relationship? What channels do they want you to use? Will those be uniform, or will they be different depending on customers and their preferences? Successful brands know how important it is to use empathy when considering these questions while creating external campaigns. They know that consumers have only so much time for any one company and realize that they will be drawn to the ones that take their time, interests, and relationships into consideration.

Memories

The final stage—and arguably the holy grail for any brand—is the imprinting of a memory in the minds of consumers. To do this, your company must know ahead of time what memory it wants to create.

Nike wants you to remember that it is there to support you, as an athlete, at any stage of your journey. Tesla wants you to think of it as the most innovative technology company in the mobility space. Amazon wants you to know that it provides you with efficiency, convenience, and choice.

These brands have done a good job establishing these memories because all of the interactions we have with them, from conversations to the eliciting of behaviors to the maintenance of our ongoing relationship, have been aligned and are in the service of creating those memories.

The establishment of a brand memory is the greatest indicator of empathic alignment between a company and consumers with a shared context. It tells us that the company and consumers understand each other, that consumers know what the company stands for, and that the company has figured out how to connect to consumers.

ONE STEP AT A TIME

We practice this three-step process—the Empathy Venn, internal alignment, and external alignment—every day with the leaders of major organizations. Each step is designed to help them understand who they are and their role in the world around them. This empathy can, and should, be applied to all facets and levels of the company as a way of bringing greater clarity, focus, and ultimately alignment to every action it takes.

Any leader who attempts to use the frameworks outlined in this chapter will undoubtedly face difficulties. Few companies are fully aligned to take advantage of the biggest growth opportunities that come their way—even the ones that are needed to make reevaluation and adjustment a part of their daily operation so they can keep up with the world around them.

The great leaders I've worked with are as obsessed with these ideas as I am. They understand their business and the ecosystem around them from every angle, putting them into a position to face challenging times and be able to build thoughtful, successful teams that are led by empathy.

CHAPTER SIX EXERCISES

Envisioning Your Future

Think about a media outlet or publication that covers your business. For financial services companies, this could include the *Wall Street Journal* or *Financial Times*. For technology companies, it might be more relevant to consider *Wired* or *Recode*. Now ask what headline you would like to see written about your company a year from now.

Some organizations want to see something about their meteoric growth or profitability. Others imagine an IPO announcement or the release of a new product that is taking the market by storm. Visualize whatever is right for you and your business, and write the headline in your journal.

The Three C's

Using the Empathy Venn, place your headline at its center and begin to consider the three C's that intersect with the headline.

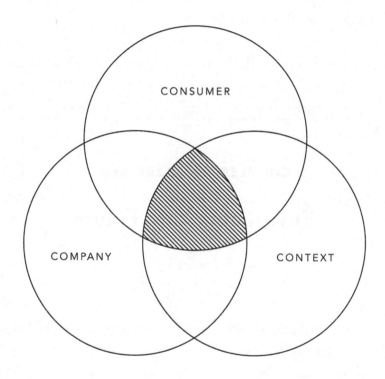

Company

Write down in one column the things your company has done and is still doing to bring this vision to life. In the neighboring column, write down a list of things your company is *not doing* or *needs to do* to make it come to fruition.

Consider your products and services, your team, your business operations, and any other elements that seem appropriate. No topic is off limits as you do this sort of work, and the more broadly you view your business, the more opportunities you will find.

Consumers

List the various consumers your company serves. Don't limit them to end consumers, but consider anyone who consumes information, products, or services produced by your business. These might include B2B partners, wholesalers, the media, financial analysts, your internal employees, and others.

Using the Empathic Archetypes, forecast how these different consumers will view your vision of the company. Wholesalers, for example, might have an easier time buying your products (or selling theirs to you). Analysts might be impressed by your company's earnings and how they will affect your shareholders. Run this exercise for each consumer group, paying attention not only to the positives that emerge but to any potential "watch-outs" or negatives that could occur should your envisioned future state come to life.

As with the company circle, put these into two columns, side by side.

Context

Ask yourself what's happening in the world around you and your business that might be relevant to your vision.

- Will advances in technology make it easier (or harder) to bring about?
- Are there regulatory concerns that may hold it back?
- Is anything happening in the cultural zeitgeist that could make the vision either more or less desirable?

What about your direct and indirect competitors? Remember the Polaroid case, and consider that competition may not come from within your industry but from a rising and disruptive industry that is parallel to your own business. Who are some companies outside of your direct competitive set that might pull the attention away from your business?

Create a list, again in two columns, of the trends that will both support and hinder the realization of your vision.

Empathic Opportunity

The center, where the three circles overlap, is your Empathic Opportunity. This is the place where your perspective and understanding of each of the C's come together to help you better comprehend the path to bring this vision to reality.

Look at the lists you've created. Do the positives outweigh the negatives? Are they almost even? If the negative columns are eclipsing the positives, you don't necessarily have to give up on your goal, but you can see how you will need to change your business in order to make it come to life.

All of this work provides you with valuable insights that will help you put together a plan that comes in the second part of this exercise.

Internal Alignment

Taking the analysis you've already done, move the empathic opportunity into the internal alignment framework.

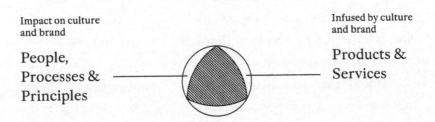

Impact on culture and brand

People, Processes & Principles

Infused by culture and brand

Products & Services

Here you can consider what you need to keep doing (or change) in order to bring your vision to life.

The left side of the graphic has three key areas of focus: people, processes, and principles, which make up your culture and behaviors.

Your first step is to evaluate your team. Do you have the right people with the right skills to get you to where you want to go? Are you carrying people who are not aligned with this vision? If so, you need to determine if they can be inspired and/or trained to be a part of the new team or if you will need to do some restructuring. It is essential that you have a team that is aligned with your vision.

Next consider the processes within your business and ask if the way they function supports your vision. Scrutinize your business from all sides, and consider where the processes need to be adjusted or reinvented.

Last, do you have the right principles? These aren't just nice words on an HR document or a website. They are the bedrock of what the company stands for. For example, if you need to behave bravely and tolerate a degree of risk to make your vision a reality, and your company has a climate of risk aversion or timidity, you may need to consider how to change that.

Map out these elements in a way that shows what you need to foster or adjust in your company's culture to get you where you want to go.

The right-hand side of the framework is for products and services. If the elements on the left have an impact on your culture and behaviors, your products and/or services are infused by your culture and behaviors.

This is when you should determine if your existing product/service portfolio is aligned with the vision you are pursuing. For instance, you may want your company to be seen as a leader in innovation, but if your internal culture is not innovative, you won't create products that are innovative. Your products and services are artifacts of your culture and behaviors. In a twist on the age-old expression "You are what you eat": "You make what you are."

Identify which of your products/services are aligned to your vision and which aren't. Take a hard look at the ones that don't align and ask yourself why you are keeping them alive.

External Alignment

When developing external alignment, there are four key aspects to consider in the way your business "shows up" in the world. They include:

- Conversations
- Behaviors
- Relationships
- Memories

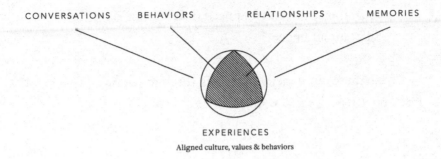

CONVERSATIONS   BEHAVIORS   RELATIONSHIPS   MEMORIES

EXPERIENCES
Aligned culture, values & behaviors

First examine these four aspects while keeping specific tactics out of your thinking. Once you establish a macro view, you can go deeper into developing specific tactics.

Conversations

These are the foundation of any external relationship your business has with the world around it. We communicate not only through our marketing and communications but also by how our brand or business shows up in our customers' or clients' lives—whether in the boardroom, in the retail environment, or perhaps on their doorstep delivered by a distributor. Every interaction is an opportunity for a meaningful conversation with your consumers.

Keeping your empathic opportunity in mind, ask yourself what conversations you need to have with people to make this vision a reality.

- What do they need to hear from you, and what do you need to hear from them?
- What channels should you use to have these conversations?
- How often should you communicate with your

consumers, and will you need different messages for different audiences?

Map these out in detail, thinking through what works best for you and the future you want to attain.

Behaviors

All conversations should have the goal of eliciting a specific behavior. People don't engage with businesses just to pass the time. It is important that you be clear what you are asking the people who interact with your brand to do.

- Why are you talking to them?
- Do you want them to buy something?
- To test-drive a new car? To tune in at 8:00 p.m. on Channel 4? To sign up for home delivery?

Understand that your conversation is meant to elicit a behavior that will support the powerful headline you imagined at the start of this exercise. Outline the behaviors you think are most critical to attaining that goal, and determine how you can encourage them.

Relationships

Your conversations and behaviors have now created a relationship. The next step is figuring out what to do with it.

Ask yourself what kind of relationship you want with your consumers. This should begin before you start your conversations.

Early planning will give you the clarity and the sense of purpose you need to bring your vision to reality.

Do you want the relationship to be daily? A news outlet should be a go-to place for what's happening in the world every day. But a luxury fashion brand, whose engagement with its consumer is higher touch and more service-minded, will need to consider a relationship that may be more infrequent but at a greater level of depth.

Take a moment to understand the relationships you want to cultivate and write down what it will take to have them.

Memories

This is the holy grail. You want to be a business that creates lasting, meaningful memories in the minds of your consumers.

When you think of a car, what is the first automotive brand that comes to your mind? Ask yourself why you thought of that one. Maybe it was the first car you owned or the one you own now. Maybe a commercial for the brand made you laugh (or cry), or maybe you drove by a billboard for the company on your way to work and the image stayed with you.

Think of the characteristics you want people to associate with your business. Make a note of them for when you review the beginning of this exercise. Keep them at the top of your mind, and let them guide your leadership and your decisions, which impact the business as a whole, making sure they align with the headline you envision. This will help make your future vision—your Empathic Opportunity—a reality.

CHAPTER SEVEN

Ritual Creates Reality

Developing your empathic abilities won't happen overnight. But as you commit yourself to thinking empathically and being empathic day after day, it will start to feel increasingly familiar. With time and dedication, you'll find that practicing empathy will become second nature. The further I've gone down the empathy rabbit hole, the more I've seen that practicing empathy not only helps us cultivate an understanding of those around us but can also give us new perspectives on ourselves and our own personal development.

To that end, our COO, Jeff, came to me one day with a provocative question that led us to a more consistent, almost ritualistic state in our practice of empathy: "What if we treated ourselves like our own best client?" he asked. "If we were to do that, what would we be doing that we're not doing now?"

As a service business, we always put our clients first, so it was a bit contrarian for us to focus on ourselves.

Jeff had already ritualized a few things around the studio that had us set up for self-evaluation. Each week we meet with different departments, which gives us a chance not only to check on specific work in progress but also to meet with each team. How are we doing? What are we struggling with? In what ways can we help one another? I know this isn't revolutionary, but it's surprising how uncommon it is. In my experiences working with companies, it's rare for executives to take the time to regularly check in with the members of their teams on a personal level and seek to truly understand how each person is doing.

A "check-in" like this might be as simple as having a cup of coffee or walking around the block together if you get the sense that someone is going through a tough time at work or at home. Such personal moments are critical to real, empathic leadership. We spend most of our professional lives working side by side with people we get to know only in a work context. The best leaders I've observed make an effort to understand what's going on with the people on their teams on a personal level—their goals, fears, hopes, and dreams; everyone has them. Time and again, I've seen great leaders do this as a way of building deeper, more meaningful relationships with the people around them.

Microsoft's CEO, Satya Nadella, is someone who is (rightly) praised for his ability to lead this way. He's brought empathy into the center of Microsoft's organization, using it as a tool to reorient the business and listen to feedback from within the company as well as the world around it. As a result, the company's internal culture, as well as its growth, is on the rise.

At Sub Rosa, we thrive on this sort of deep, personal work with our partners (Microsoft being one of them) and with ourselves. After all, if we don't understand each other, how can we expect to work well together? What Jeff was pointing out to me was that even though we had become well-practiced in doing this for our clients, we weren't doing a good enough job for ourselves. Being a service business that dedicates itself to our clients had gotten the best of us. We'd forgotten to give ourselves the same sort of attention and care. That led to the creation of Sub Rosa Day, a day each month that we dedicate fully to our internal work.

On Sub Rosa Days, there are no client meetings. No conference calls. No developing ideas for anyone else. It's one day a month when we work only on ourselves. It's fair to ask if all fifty of us are able to maintain our commitment to that every month, and the answer is no. But we make an effort to get as close to 100 percent participation as possible. On Sub Rosa Day, people can connect with colleagues they don't always interact with. We can go deep on some of the work we neglect to do on our own business—things such as project retrospectives, skills development workshops, or simply bonding with each other over a lunch or a postwork drink. Here are a few examples.

PROJECT RETROSPECTIVES

Every company has recently completed projects or initiatives that present opportunities to investigate the ins and outs of how it operates and what it does (and doesn't do) well. Looking at these in detail and evaluating them for lessons and learning are the main purpose of project retrospectives. We didn't always recognize the value of devoting time to looking at a completed project in great detail, but over time we found that doing so creates loads of interesting insights and reveals opportunities for improvement. One of our first experiences with a project retrospective was several years after our work with GE's mammography business. That study led to the Seven Archetypes and so much of our foundation in empathy.

We also discovered the value of having a project retrospective run by someone who was *not* on the project team. Such a person comes with an objectivity and lack of "tribal knowledge" about what happened on the project, and he or she is less prone to confirmation biases than the project team. This brings about inquiries whose answers reveal insights into the work that can be put to use on future projects. A person not involved with a project can also bring a fresh perspective that will provoke a team to see how they can work differently and better.

It's important to use these retrospectives to call out positives that occurred. Often retrospectives focus only on scrutinizing the shortcomings of a piece of work, but we've seen the importance of reward and recognition, giving team members the positive support they need to keep growing and doing their work better each day.

SKILLS DEVELOPMENT WORKSHOPS

Look around your organization, and ask what skills are lacking. We do this often, and a part of Sub Rosa Day focuses on training those deficiencies into strengths. Sometimes it's as straightforward as honing our presentation skills or improving a department's deftness with a particular software. But other times it has taken a more idiosyncratic and "ownable" incarnation. We utilize a basic five-step process for providing feedback. We refer to it by the acronym CLEAR:

C: Check in
L: Lead with data
E: Emotion
A: Agreement
R: Resolution

Any feedback session among team members should follow this format as a way of making sure that information and personal sentiments are shared in a manner that benefits both parties.

When we "Check in," we make sure it's the right time for feedback and all parties involved are in the right headspace to have this sort of conversation.

"Lead with data" reminds everyone to start the conversation with facts, not subjectively with feelings or opinion.

With the first two in place, it's time for "Emotion" to be revealed, with each person saying how he or she feels about a given issue or topic.

"Agreement" is a step designed to bring about common ground. You could think of this as the "empathy" step, where we look at the situation from the other person's perspective and look for the place where our views align.

We end with "Resolution," the moment when we discover how we can move forward together.

This may not be a surprising approach to conflict resolution, but interestingly, we have found it helpful to consider when there's positive feedback to deliver. Over time, CLEAR conversations have become second nature to us, and we don't always have to go through the five steps overtly because each element is integrated into our behavior. Consider your own team, culture, or company, and think about what aspects might be improved by incorporating new rituals such as these or others you might create for yourself.

Rituals such as Sub Rosa Day and CLEAR have delivered meaningful results to both our company and our culture. They foster a sense of empathy in our interpersonal relationships because they show that we are invested in taking the time to understand where each of us needs support. After all, if you can't dedicate one day a month to have your team work on itself, you're selling the company short.

This is what I mean by "ritual creates reality" in the title of this chapter. We don't create a ritual for its own sake; we ultimately want it to become so interwoven into the tapestry of our culture that our reality changes—that we become what our rituals aim to personify.

CONNECTING ONE-ON-ONE

Empathic leadership comes with some nonnegotiables. One of them is the acceptance of, and participation in, mentoring.

I'm sure that many of you have endured the rote experience of a mandated mentorship session or peer review meeting. That's not what I'm talking about here. I'm not saying that those formats can't be empathic—in fact, they *should* be; what I'm talking about is finding and connecting to people in your life who are truly valuable: people you need or who need you and with whom you can work reciprocally to give and receive feedback.

A lot of people who seek me out about their personal development do so because they think I've got it all figured out. I have learned that one of the best ways to have these conversations is to be open and honest about myself. Obviously, those people are in for a surprise when they discover how much I'm still committed to working through my own challenges. Being a leader often requires one to behave like a duck on a pond—calm and cool on the surface but kicking like hell below to keep moving forward. That's what my self-work has felt like all along, and it often still feels that way. I'm the first to admit that I don't have everything figured out, but I do know one thing about myself that has often helped guide others on their own path: empathy for myself, an ability to view my own progress as objectively as possible, has been essential to my growth.

My best mentors never forced their dogma or views onto me. Instead, they listened intently. They were curious. They worked hard to understand me and find out what I was going through. When people are mentoring, they tend to look reflexively at their own experiences and offer counsel that starts with phrases such as "When I was your age" or "Here's how I would do it." Resist that inclination when working with those around you. Though sharing a bit about your own experiences can certainly help others create new behaviors, the real gift an empathic leader can impart to someone else is a perspective on his or her own challenges so that the person being mentored can learn to see things in fresh ways.

If you consider what I do professionally, it looks kind of insane to some people. I run a fifty-person strategy and design studio; I have a thriving alternative medicine practice called Corvus Medicine; I lecture and run workshops on empathy; I teach; and my wife and I co-operate Calliope, a design-focused retail shop. To many people, that seems completely crazy, particularly because it appears to lack any real focus. But that's not how I see it.

There was a time when I felt as though I were drowning in all of those seemingly disconnected endeavors. But when a mentor of mine brought a sense of empathy and objectivity into my life, I began to see that what I do at Sub Rosa, Corvus, Calliope, and anyplace else is just the same job taking different forms. What I'm really good at is helping people identify obstacles that stand in the way of their progress and then finding solutions that remove those obstacles. Sometimes that means creating a new marketing campaign or reviving a company culture. Other times it's working a point on the body that's holding tension or lending an ear to someone who needs to unload some baggage. I've even helped a few couples who have wandered into our shop figure out how to make their house feel more like a home. Different media, same skill.

ONE CAREER, MANY JOBS

The days of working at one company for your entire career are over. In today's world, it's entirely acceptable to take multiple paths and pursue different passions across the life cycle of your career. I tell people who come to me for advice to look for consistent themes that emerge in your life and your interactions with others and to use them to push yourself toward satisfying work. For me, it was helpful to pull out wide enough to see the connective tissue across all the various things I do—to recognize that problem-solving with empathy is my core skill.

Take a moment to reflect on your life and what seems to pull you in different directions or cause you to compartmentalize yourself. What is the consistent theme or idea shared by these seemingly divergent directions? Does your career have a through line that is true for how you see yourself? These macrolevel questions can help you discover your true gifts and understand what you do that is most effective. I love to problem solve, and all of my businesses engage me in the solving of problems for others.

Problem-solving can be a bit cerebral, and I certainly appreciate that not everyone wants to fill his or her day tackling other people's challenges. Maybe you're looking to latch on to something more concrete. Perhaps you're an amazing baker or a fantastic florist. Sometimes the most empathic thing we can do for others is to point out what those gifts are and encourage others to pursue them. A few people who've passed through Sub Rosa's doors eventually determined that their passions lay elsewhere, sometimes far outside strategy and design. That's a good thing. We are all on our own path, and if being at Sub Rosa helped them discover their real passions, their true selves, it was time well spent.

I've come to believe we are all born with innate, savant-like gifts. For me it's solving problems by applying empathy, but for someone else, it might be playing the tuba. You're right to ask what the tuba has to do with this. Let me explain.

THE TUBA SAVANT THEORY

I admit the name is a bit cheeky, but what I mean is that you probably don't believe you're a savant at playing the tuba. But have you ever *tried* to play it? Maybe not. Most of us go through life playing it safe, not experimenting or trying new things. But if we want to bring empathy to ourselves and to better understand who we are and what work we're here to do, we need to experiment and discover what we're great at and then pursue it fearlessly.

I had no idea I could work in indigenous medicine or run an award-winning studio. I had to try. I had to trust that the empathy I had for myself and my innate gifts was accurate enough for me to start my own business when I was twenty-three years old and that it was a risk worth taking.

Admittedly, it's a relatively unscientific theory, but so far I've found it to be true. Everyone has powerful gifts waiting to be unlocked. Try some of the different empathic archetypes, and do some self-inquiry. See what happens when you look at yourself through the lens of the Inquirer or the Alchemist. You might be surprised to find a powerful gift waiting to be actualized.

AN INK-AND-CHEMICAL COMPANY

When we create and embrace rituals in our organizations or teams and practice them with dedication and commitment, we can bring new realities into being. This was brought home for me and my team during our work with Pantone, the creator of the Pantone Matching System, a standardized system for colors that is recognized and loved by designers worldwide. Those of you not in the design world may not be as familiar with the company, but Pantone colors are a fixture in any studio. For more than fifty years, Pantone has built a reputation as the leading color authority. Its most widely known product is a series of swatch books that enable exact color matching in the printing process.

Any big multinational company that produces marketing and promotion pieces and even, in some cases, products, depend on Pantone to be sure its brand's specific colors will be accurately printed and represented. Imagine if that iconic Coca-Cola red were printed with a lighter or darker color in different geographies. So much of the brand is built on that specific red that it would lose some of the instant recognition the company has spent decades building. But it could extend beyond that. A consumer holding a can with an off color might wonder if product quality had fallen off as well and if the drink inside were not as good as it had always been; is the off color a reflection of the company cutting corners? Such problems keep designers and brand leaders up at night. Consistency is key, and when it comes to color matching, Pantone provides its customers with confidence.

As a fan of Pantone, I was excited when, in 2014, its executive team invited us to discuss working together. A few days later, we were in a conference room with a group of company executives, and we soon figured out that they were experiencing something of a crisis of confidence. Collectively, they were concerned that the company had lost its way and were looking to define what Pantone could authentically be.

Pantone's parent company, X-Rite, Inc., had recently been acquired by Danaher, a large industrial consumer products company, which regarded Pantone as a jewel in its portfolio. Pantone had been in business for just over fifty years, and it was trying to figure out how to reposition itself for the future.

Pantone and Danaher both recognized (sadly) that print is a dying medium, and Pantone, whose business had been built with a reliance on print media, was starting to ask itself what to do next. In the United States, it holds an overwhelmingly dominant market share in its category. Almost everyone who requires color matching uses Pantone to do so.

But what does such a dominant market share mean in a declining category? If the pie is getting smaller every year, owning the whole thing matters less and less. Pantone's executives knew they had better chart a new course, or in another fifty years there wouldn't be a Pantone.

I started the meeting with a straightforward question: "How do you describe what Pantone is?"

Around the conference table every executive gave a version of the same answer: "We're an ink-and-chemical company."

Several of my colleagues from our design department were with us. We were all big fans of the company, and we were excited to get to know it better. But every time we heard "ink-and-chemical company," a little part of us died inside. We began sneaking quick "WTF?" looks at each other.

Finally one of our design leads spoke up: "An ink-and-chemical company?"

You see, to us Pantone is so much more than just ink and chemicals. It represents the integrity of design, the inspiration that comes from color, the universe of possibilities that creators can play with when developing a new campaign or product or brand.

We could see immediately that the brand had lost the spirit of what it really represented. Those executives weren't at fault; they were simply too inside their own company to see it the way we—the design community that relies on Pantone—see it. They'd lost the plot.

We knew our job was to help the employees at this company get their mojo back. We needed to help them remember why they had started working there in the first place. They needed a new perspective from which they could see the company with fresh eyes. And empathy would help us get there together.

A SPECTRUM DISORDER

We began digging into all areas of the company, from messaging and marketing to products and services, business metrics, internal culture, and more. This is how we start to understand a business without "boiling the ocean" and taking on more information than we need. It's important to build this sort of broad foundation because you never know where insights will emerge.

We spoke to employees around the world, many of whom had worked at Pantone for most of their careers. This can be both a blessing and a curse. People with long tenures may understand the business really well and possess a sort of "tribal knowledge" of the unwritten, sometimes unspoken norms of the business. But long-tenured employees can also have difficulty being objective and seeing the business from an external perspective.

The Danaher executives saw Pantone as the leader in the industry and an asset with potential for growth once the right plan was in place. But despite their enthusiasm, the team inside Pantone wasn't as optimistic. Through conversations with employees and partners of the brand, we discovered that Pantone had become a bit unwieldy in recent years. In a drive for growth, some decisions had spread the company's resources thin. It had built a licensing business, allowing partners to use the Pantone name and its iconic color swatches on consumer products. While that was a testament to the brand's strength, some of the licensing choices had not been as strategic as others. A Pantone coffee mug? Sure. Most design studios have one or two sitting around, and that's good. We discovered that it is one of the world's best-selling coffee mugs. But a Pantone roll-aboard suitcase? Maybe not so much.

We also began to understand the complexity of the company's product business. We knew how important its color matching system was in the print world, but the company also offered color accuracy products for creators ranging from interior designers to fashion and product designers.

The business is located in Carlstadt, New Jersey, along an unflattering piece of road abutting the Meadowlands (popularized on TV shows such as *The Sopranos* for its mobster-burying suitability). It is about a mile from my childhood home, and I know the area well. Only a ten-minute drive from Manhattan, it was still a world away and not at the epicenter of design culture. The location, a decidedly undesigner locale, also made recruitment and retention of top talent difficult.

The offices were a dull, buttery beige. For a company so invested in and committed to color, it seemed particularly ironic.

Those pieces of data, and others like them, were giving us a clearer picture of the real Pantone as well as a sense of where to begin our work. But we still didn't fully understand one thing about the company. We kept hearing about the Pantone Color Institute (PCI). People talked about it in meetings as though it were a mysterious, Oz-like home for color wizards. We had trouble meeting with the Color Institute people early on in our process, as they were often traveling somewhere around the world doing research, but once we were able to sit down with them, our picture of Pantone got much clearer.

AN EMERALD IN THE ROUGH

The Pantone Color Institute is made up of color experts around the globe who regularly share insights and trends they uncover from their multiple fields. They are trend forecasters in the fields of interior, graphic, product, and fashion design, and they provide information about what they are seeing and what is happening globally with color. They analyze which colors are "in" and which are "out"—which colors are gaining favor in Prague and which ones people in Singapore are sick of seeing. These people are straight-up color whisperers.

It was fascinating to see how that side of Pantone works. Our team was incredibly curious about the special sauce PCI cooks up, and we asked what the company does with all the research—how it shows up in the business. We quickly learned that much of the research goes into an annual color report that Pantone publishes and is also used to determine the "Color of the Year."

The Pantone Color of the Year is a pretty big deal. In the year we were working with them, 2013, Pantone was halfway through the year of "Emerald." The Color Institute had determined, through research and conversation, that 2013 would be a big year for emerald green. And you know what, it was right. At the fashion shows that year, pops of vibrant green were seen walking up and down the catwalks. The packaging of consumer goods saw an uptick of this jewel-like color to grab attention from shoppers looking for a new toothbrush or disposable razor. The institute had nailed it.

We were also happy to discover that the announcement of the Color of the Year was a huge media moment for the brand. News outlets and design blogs typically covered the announcement, praising the brand for its role in the creative community. The coverage is a big deal for an "ink-and-chemical company" based in the swamps of New Jersey.

Our initial research had unearthed many of the company's core elements and the ecosystem it had created. We found that about half the company's resources went to running the color-matching and swatch book business. The other half was split across licensing, marketing, and communications, the PCI, and other smaller elements. The Color of the Year was somewhat of an outlier. It didn't have a clear "owner" at the company because it ran throughout the whole company, with many departments contributing bits and pieces. It seemed odd to us that the most pressworthy part of the company occupied such a relatively small part of its mind share. Not to mention that everyone in the company, whether directly or indirectly, benefited from its being in the news.

Our close look at the Color of the Year revealed Pantone's savant gift. It was hiding right there in plain sight. The world saw it, but the company had become so locked into the day-to-day of its business that it hadn't been able to see it.

That was our way in.

We realized that the Color of the Year had more power than just being a great PR moment. Rather than being a single brick in the building, it was the mortar that could hold the company together and give it the foundation Danaher was seeking.

The Color of the Year is Applied Empathy in action. Pantone gathers its understanding of the world around it from its customers and its own internal knowledge and uses that to present a fresh perspective on the core of its business: color. It just didn't realize it was doing that.

VISUALIZING THE PAST, PRESENT, AND FUTURE

We started to think about amplifying the company's authority in the area of color intelligence. As in building a house, the most important thing is having a strong foundation. We began our work with the parent brand itself.

Pantone had used the same, straightforward logotype mark for years. It is recognizable and has a legacy we wanted to hold on to, yet we wanted to find a way to breathe new life into the brand. We suggested that if the company wanted its brand to stand for something new, an update to the brand identity would be a powerful signal that the company was undergoing an evolution.

A few weeks later, we landed on something that felt like a natural evolution; it maintained what was working, while adding something new. We kept their iconic logo but surrounded it with the outline of the Pantone swatch, placing the company's logotype inside its most recognizable symbol. We added a tagline that consumers could understand in an instant. It communicated what Pantone is here to do: Make it Brilliant.

MAKE IT BRILLIANT

"Make it Brilliant" refers not only to the company's legacy as color experts, but also to the importance of color intelligence and forecasting in its growth plan. The Sub Rosa and Pantone teams agreed that the company would have to be more than an ink-and-chemical company if it hoped to grow in the years ahead. Our work to understand the company had uncovered a clear path to the expanding of its color intelligence business.

We worked together to make the color intelligence side of the business—the insights of the experts at the Pantone Color Institute—a new year-round color intelligence business that bolstered the color matching services the company already offered. It was now monetizing these valuable data points by using them to advise other companies that wanted to make better, more informed color choices.

You might be wondering how this plays out in practice. Let's say you are part of the product design team at the Ford Motor Company. You're preparing to launch a new minivan, and you'd like to target young Millennial families. The colors of the car's exterior and interior are informed by your own research. But what if that research could be bolstered by data from the world's most renowned color experts? What if Pantone could help you see that a subtle shift in the hue of a particular color could have an impact on whether Millennial customers decide to buy the minivan? Those were the sort of powerful insights that Pantone wasn't yet monetizing but would ultimately turn into a major component of its growth plan.

The gathering of color intelligence was already a Pantone "ritual," and by applying empathy for the world of color, we helped the company turn it into something much more meaningful and momentous for the brand, which led it to develop a new reality.

TURNING A WEEK INTO A YEAR

Shortly after we created the "Make it Brilliant" brand positioning, it was time for Pantone to announce the new color of the year, and the team asked us to help them build a more empathic campaign than they'd had in years past.

The Color of the Year campaign had historically been produced on a shoestring budget. For Emerald Green, the company had used nothing more than an iconic photo of an actual emerald, set on a green background. It had milked that photo like crazy; it was on its website, on signs at trade shows, and glimmering on banner ads and social media posts. That worked okay at first, but even the finest of gemstones lose their luster, and after six months, everyone was sick of the photo but the campaign still had six more months to go.

The next year's color was Radiant Orchid, and our job was to "Make it Brilliant" with an inventive, empathic way of rolling out this new color and keeping it fresh for twelve months. Oh, and this strategy wasn't fully proven yet to Danaher, which meant we'd need to stay on a relatively shoestring budget until we had a couple wins to our credit.

We saw that Pantone's social channels were overrun with repetitive photos of that damn emerald interspersed with dry and unengaging posts that focused too much on encouraging followers to purchase new swatch books. Our research as well as our perspective on the brand told us that there were consumers out there who were desperate to interact with the brand in a more meaningful way but were not getting anything of real substance from Pantone. We began to think about doing a campaign of this scale in one studio day—all that the budget would allow—that would extend an original content story over the course of a year. We knew it would need to engage the design community and show it that Pantone was now doing things differently.

Applying empathy, we put ourselves into the perspective of the entire design community (designers, decorators, architects, and so on)—not such a stretch for a shop like ours but an important step to ensure that we were seeing the matter from all angles. We challenged ourselves to consider surprising ways Pantone could show up in the world while still being true to its brand. At the same time, we noted how often the world of design changes seasonally. Then the kernel of an idea began to emerge. We were homing in on a calendar.

With the company putting things such as color and design at the front of the conversation, we knew it had plenty of topical and timely things to say each month. But to fill a year of communications, we needed ways for it to utilize key cultural moments throughout the calendar year to bring its distinctive personality to life.

For Halloween and Thanksgiving, we had the expected images of people going trick-or-treating dressed as an orchid or a dinner table with a purple-hued turkey as the centerpiece. But that wasn't interesting enough for the creative community. The concept needed to be pushed further. We explored the strange and eccentric holidays very few of us celebrate that are quirky and playful—just like the spirit of the Pantone brand itself. Holidays such as National Squirrel Day (January 21) and Ice Cream Month (July) were just some of the ones we came upon, but if we were to fill out 365 days of content in only one studio day, we needed to get really creative.

We'd need to keep our shot list to a maximum of twelve setups in order to get the photo shoot done in one day. "Well, there *are* twelve months in a year," our design director acknowledged with a smirk. "What if we shot a single vignette for each month and cropped in different pieces depending on the content we need?"

And that's exactly what we did. We orchestrated complex vignettes for each month, made up of props and people celebrating various holidays and activities specific to that month. Pantone's social team could feed out different crops from the same photo over roughly thirty days and reveal the full vignette at the end of the month.

The content we put together was topical, idiosyncratic, and engaging. Some of it was funny, other times academic, but it was always on brand and never short on its use of Radiant Orchid to bring the imagery to life through the Color of the Year. A few weeks later, Pantone's Color of the Year was on the front page of the *Wall Street Journal* and our campaign was off to a great start.

The content we created led people to share their own "orchid moments," and it wasn't long before conversations and content were spreading all over the website. Pantone's social team was smiling from ear to ear because both sides—the folks at Pantone and their consumers—were finally understanding each other.

At the same time, the "Make it Brilliant" work was sparking new conversations, behaviors, relationships, and memories in all kinds of ways. The B2B community was appreciating the full value of Pantone's expertise in color and trend forecasting, which had already led to increased sales of the company's products and services. Those customers realized that the Pantone they had known and trusted over the years now had much more to offer. Predicated on that trust, they were willing to expand their relationship into the company's new offerings in color intelligence.

All of that new engagement and growth was bringing about a "perfect storm" of success that simultaneously enlivened the spirit of the internal culture. Over the next months, Pantone continued to see upticks in engagement, social media followership, sales, and, perhaps most exciting, team morale. With all of that work in motion, it was high time for us to make a trip back to Carlstadt.

We were blown away the minute we walked through the door and saw big printouts of the Color of the Year campaign we had produced with the company. As we were led through the main floor, we saw that more colorful printouts from the new brand book we had created were hanging on the cubicle walls. Pops of color were emerging everywhere like wildflowers in springtime.

In the conference room, we met with the same executives who only six months earlier had called Pantone an "ink-and-chemical company." Now they were beaming, asking each other things such as "Is this 'brilliant' enough?" and "How can we inspire more people with color?" Those of us from team Sub Rosa were giving one another subtle but proud head nods, realizing that we'd helped the company discover its innate gifts and ritualize some of the key behaviors and language into something that felt authentic and powerful.

MAKING BRILLIANCE A HABIT

Built into Sub Rosa is the belief that if we are doing our job well and applying empathy to solve complex problems for our partners, we should at some point create our own obsolescence. When we fix a problem, we should also deliver to the client enough tools, lessons, and empowerment that they can begin to own their own future.

This sort of thinking isn't consistent with many of the agencies in the industry, which pursue annual retainer after annual retainer, seeking the oh-so-comforting normalized cash flow we agency owners ask for in our prayers before bed.

I've always seen this differently. There are plenty of big, ambitious businesses out there with problems that need solving, so I know there's plenty more work to be had. And with a long-term retainer, at a certain point both sides start spending a lot of time managing the retainer—the agency people analyzing whether hours are burning high, pushing the agency team to the brink, or burning low and the client wondering if it is getting its money's worth. It's a constant calibration contest and a highly unempathic way of managing a partnership.

Pantone knew our philosophy on this and wanted to internalize some of the capabilities and services we were providing. We agreed wholeheartedly and locked arms with the team to help them do just that.

We worked collaboratively to identify the company's existing skills gaps and realized that it needed some new talent. But that talent would replace work we at Sub Rosa were doing. So after we helped Pantone recruit the right people, the new hires first worked for Sub Rosa for a short time in our studio, where they learned the job. After a few months, they moved full-time to the Pantone offices.

In addition, we gave a series of training sessions for existing Pantone employees to help them increase their capabilities and familiarity with the sort of work we were doing. Within about eighteen months, the Pantone team was completely empowered to do this work themselves.

It was a beautiful thing to see unfold.

The story gets a little sappy at this point, but it's the truth. One day we received the nicest letter we've ever gotten from a client, six beautiful pages from one of our key contacts at Pantone. She wrote that we had helped reinvigorate the company and ultimately ushered forth a bright new chapter for the business. She said the work we had done had singlehandedly helped retain some of the top talent within the company who had been looking toward the door.

That letter hung on our studio wall for a long time. Not only was it a nice thing to read, but, more important, it reminded us why we do what we do. When we help a company awaken and embrace its most innate gifts—when we help it realize how great it can really be—we are reminded that this is what we're here to do.

THE GREATER GOOD

Empathic leadership isn't always easy. Sometimes it is thankless and often grueling, but I know that everyone on my team has the same spirit of inspiration and hope that I do. We believe in the power of empathy as a tool to help leaders take a different view of themselves and the companies where they work. If we can do that, if we can help ignite more passion and understanding in the leaders of companies that have the largest impact on the world, we might just help create the empathic shift we all want to see in the world around us.

Every company has something special and powerful that makes it tick. If it doesn't, it's probably already out of business. Empathy is a powerful tool to identify that aspect of your own business. Talk to your customers and employees. What do they value about you and the work the company does? Task yourself with understanding what is truly special about the business. If you have a hard time discovering this, it doesn't mean it's not there.

Not all businesses are sitting on something as prominent as the Color of the Year, but there's always something you can latch on to and develop.

When you find it, treasure it. Make it a meaningful part of your business. Ritualize it by practicing it and celebrating it. Find ways to promote it in your marketing and communications. In your interviews with prospective new employees, look for it in them. Bring it to the center of your business, and let it be your North Star. Without it, you'll drift along directionless.

CHAPTER SEVEN EXERCISES

Ritualizing Empathy

Rituals can come in all shapes and sizes. This series of exercises is designed to help you understand what you are being relied upon for, as well as what you rely on most often. Exploring these will help you to dimensionalize the creation of rituals at a variety of levels for yourself and the people around you.

Personal Rituals

Take a moment to think about an aspect of yourself you'd like to nurture. Perhaps you need to give your physical body more self-care. Or maybe you want to find a regular time to decompress at the end of the day. Tune in to yourself, and see what your inner self needs. How you choose to solve this need is entirely up to you; that's not the point of the exercise. The point is to ritualize the internal check-in, to find time each day to pause and go inward, asking yourself what you need. This self-inquiry is an essential part of developing empathy for yourself, and by habitualizing this behavior, you'll find your understanding of yourself heightened over time.

One-on-One Rituals

Who are the people you interact with most regularly? Think about those relationships and ask yourself how they could be improved. Often you'll find that simply increasing your commitment to open and honest conversation—focusing on sharing your own perspectives on a particular topic—can be a simple but powerful tool to creating deeper connection. Or maybe you need the opposite: to give others the opportunity to share their perception of what they see going on. Take the time to connect with a colleague or partner, and make an effort to do this sort of work at the same time each day, week, or month. After you've spent a few sessions exploring this together, you'll likely find that the repetition and ritualization of this behavior has created a reliable structure and "safe space" for sharing with honesty.

Team Rituals

Every team has rituals, whether or not that's what they call them. Some groups have a weekly stand-up that helps to keep everyone informed and together, while others opt for a weekly happy hour to build camaraderie. Train an empathic lens on your team and ask yourself what is most lacking. Talk with other members of the team, and see what they think would be most beneficial to understanding one another. If people are craving more interpersonal/social time, find a way to create a regular series of activities that accomplishes this. On the other hand, maybe your team is yearning for more transparency. You might build a ritual around a behavior you want to use to accomplish this (e.g., encouraging the team to use a shared document or collaboration tool such as Slack to share their workload and resource constraints in real time). Again, be specific about the frequency and purpose of this new ritual, because those are the two primary ingredients necessary to having ritual create a new reality.

Encouraging Empathy

Empathy can and should be an essential part of your daily life, both in the workplace and in all of your relationships; but as we have seen, developing and applying empathy takes time and dedication.

In my own journey to apply empathy, I've discovered certain mind-sets that can help hone that ability within all of us. I look at these as "encouragements"—things we can do to inspire ourselves and the teams around us. Each one is important on its own, but collectively, they create an empathic spirit that can help you explore, learn, and grow with empathy at the center.

BE CURIOUS

Curiosity is essential. It does for empathy the same thing that sunlight and rain do for plants. It feeds empathy. Learn to be a question asker. Seek out information at every opportunity. Don't be afraid to go out on a limb in order to know someone or something more deeply. Curiosity helps us get outside of ourselves and see things from new perspectives.

But remember that curiosity can sometimes make you uncomfortable. If that happens, recognize that you're likely pushing up against some valuable sort of insight. Keep at it.

BE HONEST

Empathy requires unvarnished honesty with yourself and those around you. And it needs to receive honesty in return. If you feel you're not getting the whole truth from the people you are trying to understand more fully, you need to address that with them and find a way to create the safety necessary for it to emerge.

BE VULNERABLE

Nobody's perfect. When we attempt to present a perfect version of ourselves, we become unapproachable. People want to connect with each other on a real, human level. As a result, false perfection can often turn people off due to our apparent hubris or because it feels intimidating to them. Vulnerability comes from having the strength to know our flaws and own them when necessary. When you do this, people are able to see you for who you truly are, which gives them the confidence to share their own imperfections with you. Inside this sloppy, uncomfortable state of vulnerability is where we find the humanity within each other. Don't run from it, settle into it. You may be surprised by what you find.

BE OPEN-MINDED

Insights can come from anywhere and everywhere. If while pursuing something with empathic intuition you suspect you're headed toward a dead end—but you still have a feeling that you're on the right path—don't give up. Keep at it. Intuition and trusting in yourself are a critical part of cultivating an empathic form of leadership. Remember that being open-minded must also apply to the people with whom you are collaborating. Resist the tendency to pigeonhole them. Everyone is on his or her own journey, and you may be surprised to discover what people can do when you give them the space to connect to their inner self.

BE SELFLESS

Empathy sometimes requires selflessness. Sometimes you need to prioritize others in order to get to the right place. When people see that you've put their needs before your own, you will often find yourself in a position to lead from a place of authenticity and partnership.

Selflessness can certainly feel uncomfortable at times. Though making it a priority in the cultivation of empathy is critical, always remember to check in with your Whole Self and ensure that you are feeling aligned and balanced. Doing so provides the stability needed to act selflessly with confidence.

BE UNDETERRED

Applying empathy isn't always easy. Sometimes behaving from a place of empathy can be downright exhausting. But don't give up on it. I have seen successful leaders go to great lengths to maintain empathy for their teams, their clients, or themselves—even when it feels as though they should give up. But every time you practice empathy, using it to lead with deeper understanding or tackle challenges with more meaningful perspective, you increase your capacity to do so. Growth isn't always comfortable, but it's always expansive.

BE BRAVE

Bravery is sort of a macropoint for all of the other characteristics because you won't be able to achieve any of the others without it. But bravery isn't as hard to develop as you might think. It is almost assuredly a side effect of applying empathy, in that it involves creating the space where our skills and gifts, and those of others, can be better known. This is what gives us the courage to be brave—knowing we are supported by a deeper awareness of ourselves and the world around us.

Take these "encouragements" into consideration every day as you seek deeper understanding. Use the tools in this book when you need them, but also be open to creating your own. As your empathic instincts grow and improve, new insights will undoubtedly emerge. Trust them, and trust yourself to know what's right for you on the path ahead.

That's the true nature of empathy—it's a compass that will guide you when you need it most. Follow where it leads, and you will never be alone.

Acknowledgments

To Caroline,

I wouldn't be who I am today without you. My wife. My partner. My everything. You've taught me more about empathy than anyone else I know. Thank you. Thanks for your impeccable ability to understand me and help me to better understand the world.

To my colleagues at Sub Rosa,

Throughout the course of this book, I make mention of several of my colleagues. In addition to those mentioned, there are countless others, both present and former, who have contributed thought, discourse, and partnership to the concepts presented in this book. I'm truly grateful to all of you for the time we've shared together in our pursuit of understanding and applying empathy. This book is as much yours as it is my own.

To my editors, Matthew Benjamin and Henry Ferris,

You put me through a crash course in empathy for the editing process. It wasn't always easy, but both of you were consummate gentlemen along the way, and the ideas within this book have been made better by your partnership.

To my publishing team,

Thanks to William Morris Endeavor (especially my agent, Margaret Riley King) and the team at Simon & Schuster for your continued support and collaboration throughout this process.

To my family and friends,

Many of the lessons I've learned along the way I owe to you. My parents and sister, my friends new and old, and my teachers—your respective senses of empathy have been part of the foundation on which this work is built. Thanks for believing in me.

Index

Index

Index

Index

About the Author

Michael Ventura is the founder and CEO of Sub Rosa, a strategy and design studio that has worked with some of the world's largest and most important brands, organizations, and start-ups—from GE, Nike, Citi, and Adobe to TED, the United Nations, and the White House. Additionally, Michael has served as a board member of and adviser to a variety of organizations, including Behance, the Burning Man Project, Cooper Hewitt, and the United Nations–affiliated Tribal Link Foundation. He is also a visiting lecturer at Princeton University, where he teaches design thinking and how to integrate empathy into the creative process. In his "free time" he operates a thriving indigenous medicine practice in which he works with patients from corporate CEOs to philanthropists to help them integrate their whole selves more fully. *Applied Empathy* is his first book.